CW01501255

Echo Show 5 User Manual

450+ Tips, Tricks, Skills, Commands And
All That You Need To Know About The
Amazon Echo Show 5

Paul O. Garten

••

This book comes with a **FREE** eBook titled: **"Mastering Alexa in One Day with Over 620 Voice Commands."** It's big. It's powerful. It's rich. Don't miss it. See download link on the last page.

••

Echo Show 5 User Manual

450+ Tips, Tricks, Skills, Commands And All That You Need To Know About The Amazon Echo Show 5

Paul O. Garten

Copyright © August 2019

All rights reserved

This book or parts thereof may not be reproduced in any form, stored in a retrieval system, or transmitted in any form by any means: photocopy, electronic, recording, mechanical or otherwise without the written permission of the author.

Contents

Introduction

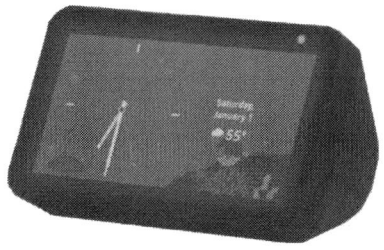

The Echo Show 5 (ES5) is comes after the Echo Show second generation released in 2018 (ES2018). The ES5 ought to be the Amazon Echo Show third generation, but the device seems to be in a class of its own. However, after seeing the first and second generation of the Echo Show, you won't be quite wrong if you refer to the ES5 as the Echo Show third generation even though the ES5 appears to be below previous Echo Show generations.

Let's face it! The ES5 can't be seen as a replacement to the ES2018, it nevertheless comes with new features and the two Shows fit for different purposes. First, it's pocket-friendly ($90) when compared to ES2018 ($230) and people who can't afford the ES2018 can still enjoy what an Amazon Echo device with a screen can offer. While the ES2018 can fit for places such as the kitchen and sitting room, the ES5 can fit for personal spaces such as a small desk, nightstand or kids' room.

The two Shows are similar in function but having a striking difference of size. While the ES2018 is 10.1," the ES5 is just 5.5." The ES5 looks more like an alarm clock whereas the ES2018 can pass for a miniature TV. The ES5 being something that fits the bedside has more clock-centric features including several clock faces and you can easily smack the top of the device to snooze the alarm.

The device also has adaptive brightness based on the environment it's placed made possible by the presence of the ambience light sensor in the device. The sunrise feature on the flipside enables the display to slowly brighten up fifteen minutes before the alarm rings in the morning. However, this feature only works when the alarm is set to ring for 4 AM to 9 AM, and not during conventional times.

The ES5 5.5" display produces a 960 x 480 resolution which seems to be okay for a smaller screen. On the whole, the video quality is just fine. The ES5 as with other Amazon Echo devices with a screen support the Amazon Prime Video, CNBC, Bloomberg and others. Sadly, you can't stream YouTube videos natively but through the built-in Firefox or Silk browsers.

You can fetch cooking recipes from sources such as AllRecipes or SideChef. You can watch instructional or DIY videos from WikiHow using the ES5. In combination with Amazon's Ring Video Doorbell, you can conveniently monitor who is at the door before opening up to them. The device also works with August doorbell cameras and Nest devices. You can also connect the device with Headspace for mindful meditations.

Unboxing the Echo Show 5 (ES5)

1.   The box comes with a 15W Power Adapter, a little guide to get you started and the ES5 smart device. The device comes in either Sandstone or Charcoal Black Color with a fabric-feel body design.

2.   Take note that the device registers to your Amazon account by default. If you are buying for someone, check the **gift option** (just below the Buy Now button) when buying it on Amazon. In any case, you can change this during setup.

Echo Show 5 vs. Echo Show 2018

More technically and comparing the ES5 with ES2018 reveals that,

3.   The ES5 has a display resolution of 960 x 480 while the ES2018 has 1280 x 800.

4.   The ES5 camera is just 1 MP, while that of ES2018 is 5 MP.

5.   The ES5 device comes with a built-in camera shutter. This feature isn't found in the ES2018. On the flipside, the ES2018 has a built-in Zigbee smart home hub for Zigbee supported devices. Such isn't found in the ES5.

6.   The WiFi connection supports the standard 802.11a/b/g/n/ac protocol. Sadly, it can't connect to a peer-to-peer WiFi network. Take note that the Echo Show 5 at this time doesn't work with Bluetooth speakers that ask for PIN codes. The device runs on MediaTek MT 8163 Processor for processing capabilities. This is same for ES2018.

Find more technical features between these two smart devices in the figures below.

The Echo Show 5 (ES5)

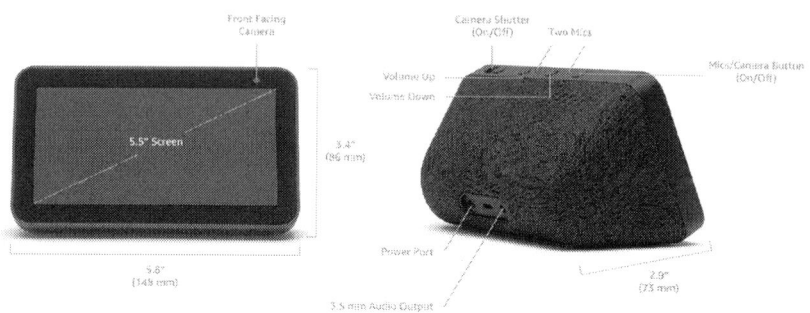

The Echo Show 2018 (ES2018)

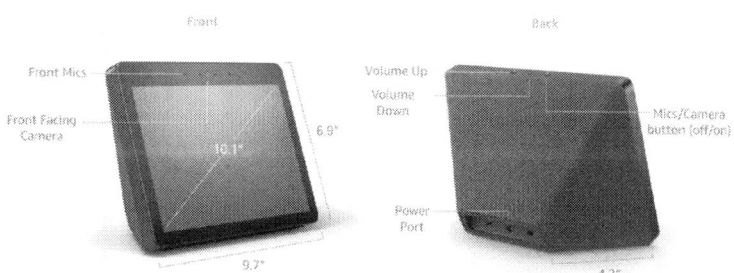

Connecting the ES5 to the Internet

7.   Connecting your Echo Show to the Internet seems to be the first thing you'll have to do once you open up the package and pull out the device and its power adapter.

8.   It's up to you where you choose to place it. If you plan to use it for surveillance, then it can fit for the sitting room so that everyone in the house can monitor it. You may choose to place it permanently in the kitchen to help with cooking but the screen seems to be too small to fit for kitchen. It can also be perfect in your bedside for alarm or monitoring the kids.

Follow the steps below to set up your device.

9.   Plug the power adapter into the power jack behind the device and plug the other end to the power outlet (mains). The ES5 powers up and setup begins. **Tip:** Keep it up to 10 meters away from the window. You can never tell, an intruder can easily send a command to the device from the window and lots can happen. Play safe! Also, don't hide it behind

anything and don't allow anything to block your voice.

10.   Select your preferred **WiFi network** and insert the **password**. Make sure you are connected to a secure network. Tap **Continue** and sign in to your Amazon account. If you don't have an account with Amazon at this time, you can visit amazon.com with your Computer or mobile phone to sign up. You can also set up a hotspot and use as your source of network.

11.   Once your Amazon account is ready, **Sign In** to your Alexa account with the details on your ES5 device, and then tap **Continue**.

12.   Confirm your **Time Zone** and **Continue**. At this point, you can change your location and time zone.

13.   The system then prompt that you place your ES5 device in a group. You may choose to **Skip** this step. You can always add the device to a group later. To learn more, see **Building a Smart Home**.

14. Note that your Echo device can only belong to one group at a time.

15. Next, name your device.

16. **Tip:** Device name could be based on location, e.g., Kitchen. Later you can have something like, "Alexa, drop in on Kitchen," or "Alexa, play music on Kitchen." Finally, tap **Continue** to see the next step.

17. Go ahead, **Download and Install** device updates.

18. **Tip:** Do this from time to time from the **Settings** to fix errors.

19. Viola! Your ES5 device is ready. Next, customization!!!

20. Go to Appstore and download your Alexa app, log in to it with your Amazon credentials and allow setup to sync it with your ES5 device. When prompted, you can start your free trial of Amazon Prime Unlimited Music, or you can set it up later by tapping **No, Thanks.** Finally, your ES5 is

ready to handle all your requests. Shortly, we'll look at how you can fully utilize the power of Alexa using the app and your voice. For now, let's customize the ES5 device.

Understanding the Light Bar Status

21.   The light ring communicates the mode of your Echo Dot to you.

22.   The device is on standby mode and awaits your request when all lights go off.

23.   The Echo Dot is starting up when a solid blue light shows with a spinning cyan light as shown below.

24. The device processes your request when a solid blue color shows while a cyan color stays and point to the direction of someone speaking to Alexa as shown below.

25. When a solid blue color alternates with cyan, the Echo Dot is responding to a request.

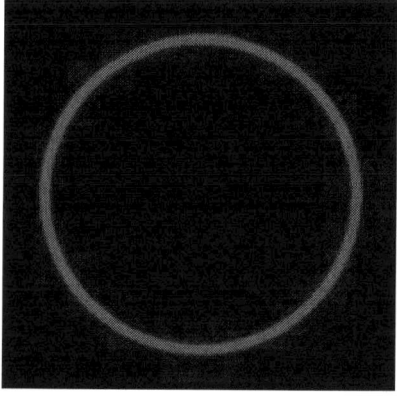

26.   A spinning orange color light in a clockwise direction shows that the Echo Dot is connecting to the internet through your WiFi network as depicted below.

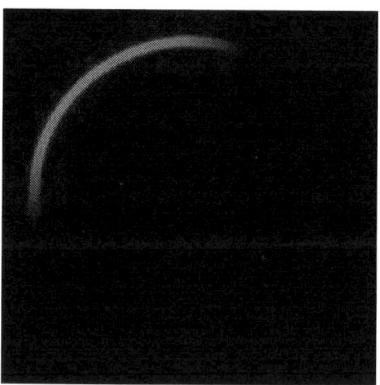

27.   When the microphones are turned off, the Echo device shows a solid red light. You can always turn on the microphones by pressing the **Microphone** button. See the illustration below.

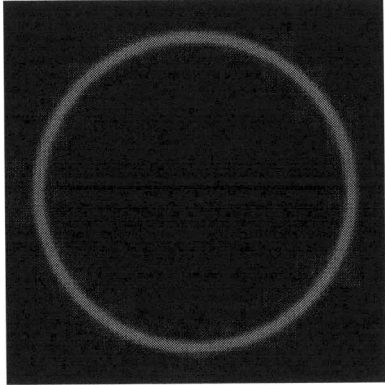

28.   A pulsing yellow color light shows that you have a message or notification. You can access them by saying, "Alexa, what messages do I have?" or "Alexa, what notifications do I have?"

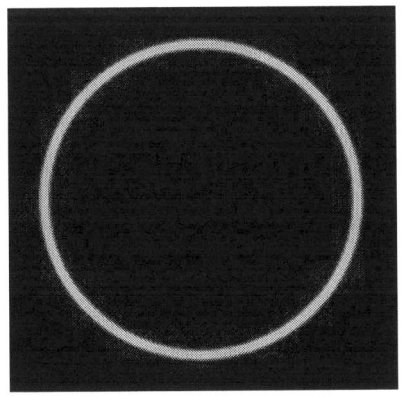

29.   A pulsing green color light shows a Drop In action, or it means you are receiving a call.

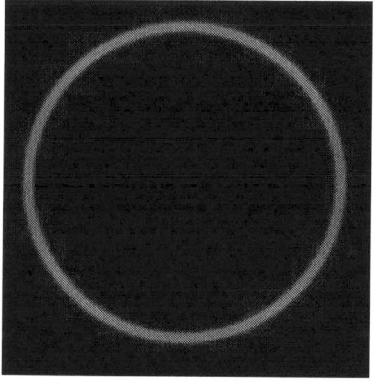

30.   When a green color light spins clockwise, it means the Echo Dot is making a call, or you are Dropping In on another person's device.

31.   Volume adjustment action shows a white light on the device.

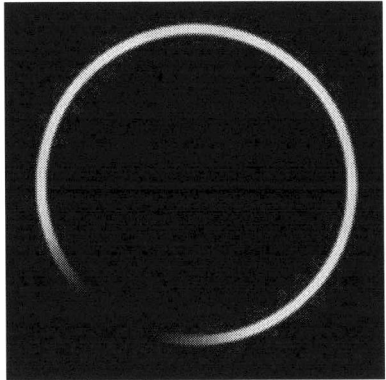

32.   During WiFi setup, a continuous pulsing violet color light shows that an error has occurred. Repeat the process.

33.   A purple flash light after interacting with Alexa shows that the Do Not Disturb feature is enabled.

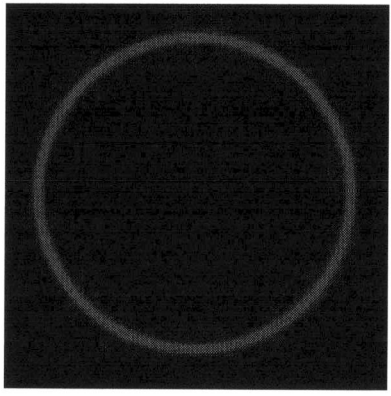

Customizing the ES5

The Home Screen

Swiping down from the top of the screen shows four main buttons: the Home button, the screen brightness control bar, the Do Not Disturb (DND) button, and the Settings button.

34. The **Home button** when tapped would always take you to the homepage from anywhere you are within the device. Alternatively, you can say, "Alexa, go home."

35. Adjusting the brightness bar to the left reduces the screen brightness and to the right

increases it. You can also do this from the **Settings**.

36. Activating the DND would reject incoming calls and Drop Ins but permitting only the alarm and timers. To learn more about Drop In, see **Alexa Communications.**

37. Tapping on Settings take you to the settings page where you can customize your device. You can also say, "Alexa, go to settings."

Exploring the Settings

The **Settings** show customization options for Bluetooth, WiFi network, Home & Clock, Display, Sounds, DND, Communications, Device Options, Restrict Access, Things to Try, and Legal.

Home & Clock

Under **Home & Clock,**

38. You can set how you want your clock and home screen to appear.

39. You can also manage the **Home Content**, i.e., the things that show on your home screen. Toggle **Rotate Continuously** to the right to continuously rotate your home contents. **Allowing the toggle to stay by left puts off all the annoying ads and "things to try" that continuously rotate on the home screen**. Don't forget to tap and set the **Displayed Content** that you want to rotate on the home screen.

40. If you want Alexa to be giving you tips on how to get the best of her, toggle **Discovery** to the right.

41. Toggle **Drop In** to the right to **Enable** it and be able to see recently active Drop In contacts. More on this later.

You can also toggle ON / OFF:

42. **Final Scores** for your favorite sports or teams set up under your **Flash Briefings** in the Alexa app.

43. **Notification** from skills enabled for your device.

44. **Photo Highlights** from your "This Day" photos on Amazon.

45. **Upcoming Reminders** that you set on your device to remind you what's next.

46. **Shared With You** photos from your family and friends on Amazon.

47. **Stock** quotes from connected services.

48. **Trending Topics** from Amazon.

49. **Upcoming Events** you've created and added to your calendar.

50. **Upcoming Games** to alert you on when your teams are playing.

51. **Weather Alerts** to keep in tune with the weather conditions in your area.

52.   **Weather Forecast** will furnish you with information concerning your local and international weather forecast.

Display

Under **Display**, you have options to,

Setting Up a Photo Slideshow

53.   Set up a slideshow of your photos. To begin, tap **Photo Slideshow** to select your photos.

Setting the Brightness

54.   The **Brightness Bar** is there so you can adjust the screen brightness. As said earlier, you can move the bar left or right to decrease or increase the screen brightness.

Setting the Adaptive Brightness

55.   Toggling the **Adaptive Brightness** to the right would automatically adjust the screen brightness based on the surrounding light.

Setting the Sunrise Effect

56.   The **Sunrise Effect** when toggled on would make the screen to gradually lighten up in a sunrise manner when the alarm is set to ring for 4 AM - 9 AM.

Night Mode

Under **Night Mode**, you can,

57.   Set the device to **Night Mode** which deems the clock face when lights are turned off in the room. To begin, tap **Night Mode** and toggle **Nighttime Clock** to right.

58.   Two options exist for putting the clock on night mode. You can manually **Schedule** when the night mode should occur. Feel free to set your range, e.g., 10 PM - 7 AM, or,

59. Set the clock to automatically enter night mode when there's no light in the room.

60. If you wish, you can toggle to the right to use the clock to **24-Hour Clock** instead of 12.

Connecting External Wireless / Bluetooth Devices

61. Under **Bluetooth**, you can pair the ES5 with any devices. Once you are there, the system shows available Bluetooth devices near you which you can easily tap to create a connection with them. For example, to connect your phone, turn ON your phone's Bluetooth and tap on it once the ES5 can detect it. From there, you can play music from the phone once and control it using the device, Alexa, or the phone.

62. In a similar manner, you can also connect a wireless / Bluetooth speaker with the device for a better sound quality. Take your Bluetooth device connection with the ES5 one at a time! Set them 5 ft. apart. Once your Bluetooth speaker is ready, power it on and raise the volume. Next, set your

Bluetooth speaker on pairing mode. Go to the Alexa application, under **Settings**, tap **Devices**.

63.   You can also access the **Devices** icon from the Alexa homepage/screen. Choose your Echo device, select **Bluetooth Devices** and **Pair a New Device**. From the list of devices that shows, choose your Bluetooth speaker. Follow the onscreen instructions to complete the process. If your Bluetooth speaker has been paired already before this time, simply say, "Alexa, connect."

64.   **Tip:** Always go for a certified smart speaker to work with the Amazon Echo devices to avoid issues.

Sound Settings

Under **Sounds**,

65.   Adjusting the **Media** bar left or right set the volume of the device to low, medium, or high as the case may be when playing media contents.

66. The **Equalizer** takes care of how you want the sound coming out from the device to be. Here, you adjust the Bass, Mid, or Treble.

Notification Settings

67. You can also set the volume level for your **Alarms, Timers and Notifications** using the third option.

68. Toggling the **Ascending Alarm** to the right gradually raises the alarm volume until it reaches your selected level.

69. You can control what notification you get on your ES5 using the Alexa app. To get started, go to **Settings > Alexa Account > Notifications**. Under **Amazon**, select a feature to see notification options.

70. To turn on/off notifications for any selected skill, go to **Settings** and then **Notifications**.

71. To manage notifications from your Alexa skills, tap the **Menu** ☰ icon and select **Skills & Games**. Select a skill from the **Your Skills** tab to edit notifications options. Tap **Manage Permissions** and toggle to **On / Off** notifications.

72. When you see a notification banner on the home screen, say, "Alexa, read my notifications" to read them and while that's going on, you can say, "Alexa, [next / previous] notification."

73. To clear all notifications, say, "Alexa, remove all my notifications."

74. To manage your notification sounds, tap **Devices** on the Alexa app homepage and select your Echo device. Select **Sounds** and navigate to the **Notifications** area. Tap on **Notifications**; to mute notification sound, select **None**.

Under **Custom Sounds,**

75. You can set your preferred sound for the **Alarms**. To begin, tap **Alarms** and select your preferred sound from the list and then

tap the little arrow on the top left to see your previous screen.

76.   Choose either **Default** or **None** for your **Notifications** sound.

77.   The **Request Sounds** plays a sound when you make a request from Alexa. You can toggle to hear a sound at **Start** and **End of Request**.

Do Not Disturb (DND)

Under **Do Not Disturb (DND),** you can,

78.   Toggling the first option (Do Not Disturb) to the right stops all your notifications (calls, messages, announcements, and Drop Ins) from coming in except for alarms and timers.

79.   Toggling the second option would help you to set a **Recurring DND** on a daily basis for selected **Starts** and **End time**. For example, you can set a recurring DND for your daily prayer times.

80. To schedule a DND action from the Alexa mobile app, tap the **Devices** 🏠 icon and select your **Echo device** then **Do Not Disturb**. Toggle it **On.** You can also **Schedule** the **Start** and **End** times for your Drop In on a daily basis. Tap **Done** to save your changes.

81. A quick way to go about this is toggling on the DND icon on the Home Screen to On/Off. Swipe down from the screen top to see the **Do Not Disturb** button.

Communication Settings

Under **Communications,**

82. You have an option to toggle the **Incoming Call Ringer** to ON / OFF, i.e., allowing or disallowing the device to ring when there's an incoming call.

Device Options

Under **Device Options,**

83. You can change your **Device Name** from the displayed name to any name that

you want. **Tip:** You can name your Echo device based on location, e.g., Kids Room, Kitchen, etc.

84. To change your Echo device name from the Alexa app, tap on the **Menu** and then **Settings**. From Settings, choose the Echo device that you want to rename and tap on **Edit** against the device's name. Enter new device name and **Save**.

85. To rename your smart home devices, tap the **Menu** and then select **Smart Home**. From the list, tap the smart device you want to rename and then the ellipses icon and **Edit Name** [Note that you can also disable a device on this page by toggling the **Enabled** button to disabled it]. Hit **Done** to save your new device name.

86. Take note that you are only renaming the device for Alexa only. It is advisable that you also rename the device from its companion app (if any).

Setting Your Location

87. Set your **Device Location** from the second option any time you change your location.

88. You can also change your device location from the Alexa app. Your location is very important to Alexa as uses it to personalize your experience for services such as local searches, weather, shopping, time and other specific local features. To change your location in the Alexa app, tap the **Devices** 🏠 icon on the homepage, select your ES5 device and tap **Device Location**. Type in your address and **Save**.

89. If more than one Echo device is connected to your account, you'll have to update their location one after the other.

Setting Your Device Language

90. You can also set your **Device Language** using the third option.

Setting Your ES5 Wake Word

91.   This option takes care of the wake word you wish to attach to your device that connects the device to the Amazon cloud service to process all your requests. For all Amazon Echo devices, the default Wake Word is Alexa. As such, if you have more than one Amazon Echo device in the house, you can't have all their Wake Words to be Alexa. You'd be creating confusion. On this note, apart from Alexa, you can change the **Wake Word** to **Echo, Amazon,** or **Computer**.

92.   **Tip:** If your Echo devices are far apart such that one can't hear the other, you can still choose Alexa as their wake word.

93.   To change the wake word from the Alexa app, tap **Devices** from the homepage, select your Echo Show 5 and tap **Wake Word.** From the list, you can change to Amazon, Computer or Echo. Select **OK** to save when done. During this time, the device cannot process any request until the wake word is fully activated.

94.   To initiate the process with your voice, say, "Alexa, change my Wake Word."

Tap Gestures

95.   If toggled ON, the **Tap Gestures** allows you to smack the top of the ES5 device to snooze the alarm.

Date and Time Settings

96.   Tap **Date & Time** to set the date and time by setting your region and time zone.

Measuring Units

97.   The **Temperature** measuring unit is set to Fahrenheit by default. You can change this here.

98.   **Distance** is set to miles by default. You can also change this as well.

Web Options

Under **Web Options,**

99. Tap **Browser** to tune **Browser Settings** for your **Silk** or **Firefox** browsers. You can also tap the radio button to set any of them as default.

100. Tap **Web Videos** to **Clear Cache** or **Clear Cookies**. At this time, there's actually nothing to clear.

101. **Tip:** A web cache stores web pages, images, and other web multimedia to reduce page load time or server lag; while web cookies remembers a web user's browsing activity. Web cookies are usually a tiny piece of data when compared to caches.

Connecting Your Echo Remote and other Gadgets

102. Use the next option to **Pair Amazon Echo Remote** with your ES5 device to enable you control media playback on the device.

103. From the Alexa app, tap **Devices** , select your ES5 device and then **Pair Amazon Echo Remote**. Insert your batteries, press and hold down the Play button for seconds. A confirmation message comes after 40 seconds or less that the remote has been paired.

104. You can also **Pair Alexa Gadget** such as Echo button for games.

Device Updates

105. From time to time, you can **Check for Software Updates** to fix errors on the device or access new features.

Resetting Your ES5 Device

106. Maybe you want to give out your ES5 to someone else, you can tap on the option to restore it **Factory Settings** so that the person can start afresh to use it.

Parental Control

Under **Restrict Access,**

107. Toggling **Amazon Photos** to the right restrict users from viewing your Amazon Photos. Note that you may not be able to use them as home screen background photo.

108. Toggling **Movie Trailers** to the right restrict users from using the device to search and watch movie trailers.

109. Toggling **Web Browsers** to the right restrict users from using the device to perform web searches.

110. Toggling **Web Video Search** to the right restrict users from using the device to search videos.

111. Toggling **Video Providers** to the right restrict enabled video providers on the device.

These restriction options are particularly important to keep kids away from accessing contents you may not want them to see.

112. The **Things To Try** contains a list of things to try with your ES5. Start by calling Alexa and then say any of the things on the list. Example, "Alexa, call mom."

Accessibility Settings

Under **Accessibility,**

113. For **Vision**, you can toggle ON your ability to use gestures and magnify the screen via **Screen Magnifier.**

114. You can also toggle to **Invert** or **Correct** the screen color. But note that color inversion may affect device performance.

115. Toggling **Closed Captioning** to the right would show captions (sub-title) for videos where available.

116. Toggling **Alexa Captioning** to the right would show captions for Alexa responses when available.

117. When you don't want to ask Alexa your favorite things by voice, you can do that via touch when you enable **Tap to Alexa.**

118. You can also toggle the **Calling and Messaging Without Speech** to the right to see transcript for received messages.

119. **Tip:** Don't forget to always tap on the little arrow **<** pointing back on the top left corner of the screen anytime you are done with making settings on a page. At any point, you can swipe the screen from the top and tap on the Home button to go to the home page.

The ES5 Side Menu (Alexa app)

120. Swiping from the **right side of the screen** shows a portable Alexa app installed on the ES5. The app contains options that you can quickly use to work with your ES5 device instead of going to your mobile phone to use the Alexa app.

On the screen, we have options for Communication, Smart Home, Music, Video, Routine, and Alarm.

Alexa Communication

Under **Communication**, we have Drop In, Announce, Call, Message, and Show Contacts.

Drop In

121. Drop In can grant you access to other Amazon Echo devices in your home or those of your connected contacts that have enabled you to Drop In on them. If you enable them, they can also Drop In on you.

122. You can start an audio or video conversation with another user of Alexa Drop In enabled device. They don't always have to permit you to bump into them once they've enabled you to Drop In on them. This is different from the conventional calls that you can choose to receive, ignore or reject an incoming call.

123. To begin, tap **Drop In** to see devices or contacts that you can Drop In. From here, you can tap on any device on the list to begin a Drop In session with them.

124. Dropping in on Echo devices without a screen only returns audio feed from what's going on in that location.

125. **Tip:** Since this comes unannounced, you can choose to disable it to avoid someone popping into your privacy.

126. To enable or disable Drop In using the Alexa mobile app, tap the **Menu** 🗐 icon, go to **Settings** and select the device you want to enable or disable the Drop In function. Tap the Drop In menu and tune it the way you want from there. You have options to **enable** [On] meaning that your contacts that you've enabled Drop In for can always Drop In on you as well as other Echo devices within your home. **Allowing it work within your home** means that only Amazon Echo devices within your home can Drop In on you. You can also **disable** [Off] it completely if you are not comfortable with the Drop In feature. To try this out after enabling the feature, say, "Alexa,

Drop In on the Kitchen," where **Kitchen** is the name of the Echo device stationed there.

127. To enable or disable Drop In for any particular contact, from your Alexa app, tap **Communication** and then **Contacts** , tap a contact and under **Permissions**, toggle **Allow Drop In** to the right.

128. Under **Information**, you can tap **Block Contact** to completely block the contact and their household from reaching you via Alexa calling and messaging.

Sending Announcement

129. The Announce feature broadcast a one-way message to all Amazon Echo devices in your house. You can use either use the keywords, 'Announce' or 'Broadcast' to begin a broadcast message. Example, "Alexa, announce that we are leaving by 3 PM." You can also say, "Alexa, broadcast someone should feed the puppy."

130. Using the Alexa app, under **Communication**, tap **Announce** then **type** or tap the **microphone** button to say your message. Tap same button to broadcast your message to all connected Echo devices in your home.

Messaging

Once you've set up your Alexa app for conversations or communication, you can begin to send SMS to your Alexa contacts. You can send messages to family and friends using your Echo Show device.

131. From your Alexa app, tap on the **Communication** button and then, **Contacts.** Tap on **My Profile** and under **Permission,** toggle on **Send SMS** and you are good to go. **Allow** Alexa to send and read SMS. That's all the set up you need to do for the first time to enable messaging using the app.

132. The command here is simple: "Alexa, send a text message," "Alexa, send an SMS." Alexa would then request for a contact within

your Alexa app. Go ahead and say your message and leave the remaining for Alexa.

133. You can also save Alexa some stress by using a command such as: "Alexa, send a text message to <your Alexa contact name> or "Alexa, send an SMS to <your Alexa contact name>."

134. To send a message within the Alexa app, tap **Communication** and then **Contact**. Select a contact from the list and tap the **Messaging** button .

135. A dot on the **Communication** button shows you have a new message. You also get a notification on your ES5 home screen.

136. For best result with messaging, your recipient must be on the same mobile operating system with you.

137. You can't send an SMS to 911, or groups.

138. You can't also send an MMS with this setup.

Video / Audio Calls

139. You can make free calls to other Echo devices or contacts on your Alexa app that support this feature. To begin, launch your Alexa app and tap on the **Communication**. Tap on the **Contacts.** Grant Alexa all necessary permissions when requested. All contacts you can call would be displayed here. You can tap on any to see their info. Right there, you can make an audio 📞 or video 📹 call to them by tapping the right button on the contact page.

140. Using a voice invocation, you can say, "Alexa, call Garten," "Alexa, video off" [that's if she's trying to video call by default]. You can also say, "Alexa, call video call Garten." Once you are done, say, "Alexa, end call." You can as well tap on the **Hang Up** icon on the screen to end a call or simply say, "Alexa, hang up."

141. To answer or ignore your Alexa-to-Alexa incoming calls to your Echo, say, "Alexa, answer," or "Alexa, ignore." You can also use the DND feature to block or ignore calls.

142. You can use the camera shutter to close the camera during a video call session and block the other person from seeing you.

E-mailing

143. You can link your email accounts and have Alexa help you to manage it. Before continuing, note that anyone that gain access to your Echo devices can access your emails. You can connect up to 3 e-mail addresses to your Alexa account. Your adult Household Member can also do same. Set and use a voice PIN to safeguard your e-mail from unauthorized access.

144. To link an account, launch the Alexa app and go to **Settings**, tap **Email & Calendar**. See list of providers supported by Alexa and choose one to setup. Supply login details and grant Alexa access. Alexa report on your email activities for the last 24 hrs.

Some useful invocations for e-mail

145. To see new emails, say "Alexa, show my e-mail," "Alexa, what's my mail?," "Alexa, open my mail."

146. To find out if a particular contact sent you a mail, say, "Alexa, did <sender name> send me any e-mails?"

147. To read / listen to content, say "Alexa, play new messages."

148. To reply: "Alexa, reply."

149. To skip an email: "Alexa, skip."

150. To delete: "Alexa, delete it."

Setting a Household Profile

A Household Profile enables you to share contents (e.g., audiobooks, calendars, music, etc.), manage account features (e.g., to-do lists, shopping list, etc.) and access customized content (e.g., traffic, news). The Amazon Household Profile settings permit 2 adults Amazon accounts and up to 4 child accounts. While adult accounts can be added directly through the app, the child accounts can only be added through **FreeTime**.

151. To create a Household Profile, open your Alexa app, tap **Menu** ☰ and go to **Settings** > **Alexa Account** > **Amazon Household**.

152. Begin the process by tapping **Start** to add a household member. Alexa prompt you to **Pass Your Device** to the person that would like to join your household so that they can sign in to their account. If they are not available, you can get their username and password to complete the process on their behalf then have them **Join Household** and finally, the **Household is Created**.

153. The new person added needs to complete the process by logging into the Alexa app. You can sign out and allow them sign in with their details using your device to complete the process.

154. Adding a Child Account would require you go through FreeTime. In the Alexa app and from **Menu** ▤, go to **Settings**, and tap on the Echo device meant for this to get started. Find **FreeTime** under **General**. In **FreeTime Settings**, toggle it to **Enable**. **Setup Amazon FreeTime** by **Enabling** desired features just by toggling them and **Continue** when done.

155. Manage your Child's Profile at **Parent's Dashboard** using the link: **Take Me to Parent's Dashboard.** At Parent's Dashboard, you can monitor your child's activities and adjust what features the child can access.

156. To switch between accounts, say, "Alexa, switch <account name> account." The new person takes charge of Alexa. While this works only for adult account; to switch to a child's account, the FreeTime feature must be turned ON, and OFF when going back to an

adult account. See FreeTime Settings to Enable or Disable it.

157. Once FreeTime is turned OFF, the account switches to previous adult that used the device. You can always find out whose account you are using by saying, "Alexa, whose account is this?"

158. A second adult added to your Amazon Household can actually use your payment method to buy from Amazon and also view your Prime Photos.

159. Since you'll be possibly sharing your Amazon profile, it is advisable that you create a Confirmation Code for your voice purchases.

160. To switch between profiles, just say, "Alexa, switch accounts."

161. To check user profile, ask, "Alexa, which account am I using?"

To delete a household profile

162. Go to Amazon Household in the Alexa mobile app and select **Remove** against the user's profile. If it's you, tap **Leave**.

Managing Your Photos

163. You can take photos using the camera on your Echo device and also view a slideshow of them on the Screen. To set slideshow speed, swipe down the screen and tap **Settings**. Alternatively, say, "Alexa, show Settings." From **Settings**, tap **Display** and finally **Photo Slideshow**. Tapping on **Photo Slideshow** would take you to **Photo Preferences** where you can set your preferred slideshow speed.

164. To take a shot, say, "Alexa, take a shot." Your photos are immediately posted to your account.

165. You can also share your photos from your Amazon account with your contacts in the Alexa app. To share a photo while viewing it, say, "Alexa, share this photo to

<Alexa contact name>" or "Alexa, send this photo to <Alexa contact name>." Your recipient would get an email informing them about shared photos.

More useful invocations for photos

166. To see your photos: "Alexa, show my photos."

167. To specify location/album: "Alexa, show my Family Vault photos" or "Alexa, show my This Day photos" or "Alexa, show my <album name> album."

168. To show your albums: "Alexa, show all my photo albums."

169. To control slideshow: "Alexa, [pause / repeat / resume] slideshow,"

170. "Alexa, [next / previous] photo," "Alexa, turn [on / off] shuffle."

171. "Alexa, zoom [out / in] photo.

172. To view photo using criteria: "Alexa, show my photos of Forest," "Alexa, show photos of Germany," "Alexa, show beach photos" or "Alexa, show photos of last year."

173. To see shared photos: "Alexa, show John's shared photos," "Alexa, show photos from Lizzy" or "Alexa, show photos sent by Paul."

174. To take a picture: "Alexa, take a picture of me."

175. To see a random picture about something: "Alexa, show me a Dog picture."

Building a Smart Home

176. For a smooth communication between your smart home devices with Alexa app, make sure the device shares the same WiFi network with the ES5 device.

177. **Tip:** Once Alexa is enabled for devices, anyone voicing the right command can get Alexa to trigger the connected or concerned

devices to work. Anyone can also control your Smart Home devices through the Alexa app installed on your phone. As a way of controlling who can send commands to Alexa or control your smart home devices, put the microphones off when away from home and also protect your phone with a PIN code.

178. To connect your smart home device using a Skill, power on the device and enable the associated skill via **Menu > Skills**. See case study with a smart home Camera below.

Configuring Your Smart Home Cameras with Alexa and Other Devices

179. When making an order for a smart device with intention of pairing same to Amazon Alexa, make sure that such a device is certified by Amazon to be compatible with Alexa. Follow the link here to browse through Amazon recommendations in this regard: https://amzn.to/2R8WK7J.

180. Connect your smart camera through the exact WiFi network your Amazon smart devices are using.

181. In the Alexa application, go to **Menu** ▤ and tap on **Skills.** Tap the Search ▣ icon to enter the skill name and then search for it. Locate your associated camera skill from the search result and **Enable** it. **Sign In** to your account with them if necessary.

182. Next, tap the **Home** ▤button, **Devices** ▥, and then tap the **Plus sign** ⊕ and select **Add Device** from the ensuing menu. Under **All Devices**, select **Camera** [for our case here], and then your brand of camera, e.g., Ring, Nest, etc. Next, download the camera or device app from manufacturer's website, Play or App Store and set up the camera following the instructions coming from the app. Once you are done doing that, go back to the Alexa app and tap **Continue**. Finally, your camera is ready and registered under **Devices** in Alexa app. Adding any other smart home device follow similar process.

183. To use your newly added camera, you can say, "Alexa, show the Front Door," where **Front Door** is the name of your camera.

184. **Tip:** The Ring Doorbell has the **Microphone ON** advantage over Nest Doorbell. You can actually communicate with whoever is at the door, but you can't do that with a Nest camera.

185. You can request for live feeds from Alexa using the format: "Alexa, show [event / live video feed] from <camera name>."

186. You can also request for past feeds depending on your location or the nature of your security camera by saying, "Alexa, show the latest feed from <camera name>."

187. Most smart devices work two ways: ON / OFF. Hence, we can have something like, "Alexa, turn [on / off] Office," where **Office** refer to the name of your smart bulb group in your office.

188. You can also open a smart home group containing two or more devices and tap to turn ON / OFF a specific device within the group.

189. From **Devices** , you can simply tap on your smart device to switch it ON / OFF, UP / DOWN, HIGH / LOW, etc.

190. You can also switch any of your smart devices individually using your voice, e.g., "Alexa, switch [on / off] Living Room."

Creating a Group for Your Smart Home Devices

191. Placing your device in a group can help you to control them using a single command.

192. Your ES5 device comes with predefined groups such as Christmas Lights, Downstairs, Family Room, Kids Room, Living Room, Office, and Toy Room.

193. From the Alexa app, tap the **Devices** button, open any of the predefined groups and then tap the **plus** icon to add a smart device. Such device must have been added to the Alexa app before now.

194. You can also add a custom group by selecting **Add group** via **Devices** > **Plus Sign** ⊕ > **Add Group**. Enter your preferred group name, then tap **Next** and choose preferred devices for the group, finally, **Save.** Once you set up a device for your group, you can easily pass a voice command that'll affect all members of the group at once and you can always edit the group's items, i.e. add or remove a device from there.

195. For this nature of setup, you can easily say, "Alexa, turn on <smart device group name>" or Alexa, play Don Moen on <smart device group name> where smart group devices may be 5 smart security light bulbs, 3 wall plugs or 2 smart speakers. However, your Echo device can only be linked to a smart group at one time.

196. Alternatively, visit alexa.amazon.com. Click on **Smart Home** > **Groups** > **Create Group**. Enter a name for your group and then mark the devices you want to add to the group. Finally, click Save. All groups created using a computer within the same Amazon account also appears in your Alexa app.

How to delete / edit a smart home group

197. To delete / edit a smart group, open it within the **Smart Home** tab via **alexa.amazon.com**, click on **Groups** and then click on the group you want to delete / edit its contents.

198. To edit, mark [or tick] more devices for the group or unmark the ones you wish to take out of the group. You can also change the group's name. Finally, click **Save**. To delete, click on **Delete this group** and confirm your decision.

199. Alternatively, in the Alexa app, you can always add or remove members to/from a smart home group after creating it. To get started, from the Alexa app home page, tap the **Devices** icon. Select a smart home group to edit and then tap **Edit** (see top right-hand corner). Next, **Edit Name**. You can simply pick a pre-defined name or enter your own name. Tap **Next**. Select the group's devices and then **Save**. To completely remove the group, hit the **Trash Can** icon (see top right-hand corner). Note that you can delete and reuse a group's name. If facing challenges

re-using a group's name, uninstall and reinstall the Alexa app.

200. If you've added a smart lock to your Alexa app, you can say, "Alexa, [lock / unlock] the '**front door,**'" where 'front door' is the name of your smart lock.

201. For a Thermostat, you can say, "Alexa, what's the temperature of the Thermostat."

202. To check the thermostat, "Alexa, what's the temperature of the thermostat?," or "Alexa, set the thermostat to <#> degrees."

203. For a smart bulb, you can say, "Alexa, dim [or brighten] '**bedroom light**'," where bedroom light is your Philip Hue smart bulb.

204. To turn an activity or a channel on, "Alexa, turn on activity / channel."

205. To speed up or slow your fan, "Alexa, set fan speed in <fan location name> to <#> percent."

206. To check your doors, "Alexa, is the [front / back] door locked?"

207. For your microwave, "Alexa, set the microwave for <#> minutes."

208. **Tip:** Set up a code for unlocking your doors when enabling "Unlock by Voice" Alexa skill for your doors.

How to Create a Scene

209. Creating a Scene requires that you first of all set up the Scene within your smart device companion application. For example, if you intend creating a Scene to have the Philips Hue light deemed when the Scene is triggered, then you will first of all set up the Scene in the Philips Hue mobile app. Same goes for other smart devices.

210. Once that is done, using your computer via alexa.amazon.com, and in the **Smart Home** tab, click on Scenes. All the **Scenes** that you've created for your smart devices would appear here. If you don't find them, click **Discover**. Scenes are controlled based on the name you gave to them and they still work by

switching. Example, "Alexa, turn on 'nighttime'." Where 'nighttime' is the name of the Scene.

211. To delete a Scene, open the Scene from the **Smart Home** tab and then click on **Forget**.

Linking Your Bluetooth Speaker / Home Stereo System with Your Echo Show

212. Pairing your Bluetooth speaker means that you have connected your Echo device to Alexa before this time and hence linking a Bluetooth speaker to the Echo device. Linking a smart speaker to your Echo device is especially important if you want to improve the sound quality of your Echo speaker and hence, connecting an external speaker to it via Bluetooth or using an audio cable.

213. To pair a Bluetooth speaker, keep the speaker 3—5 feet away from your Echo Show and tune it to be on pairing mode. Next, go to the Alexa mobile app and tap **Menu**, from **Settings**, select your Echo Studio, and then **Bluetooth**. Allow scanning to be

completed then choose your Bluetooth speaker and finally, you are done setting up your speaker.

214. To connect your Echo Show to your home stereo system, use a 3.5mm audio output to connect the two together. You can also connect your wired headphone to your Echo device by plugging in the 3.5mm headphone input to the AUX audio output of your Echo Dot (see the audio jack behind the device).

Linking Your Smart Home Devices via Zigbee Hub

215. Where the Zigbee hub is available, you can seamlessly link supported smart devices to Alexa.

216. Follow the steps below to link your devices.

217. Keep your smart device ready to be linked within a 30 feet distance from your Echo Show.

218. Make sure that the device is powered on. Next, say, "Alexa, discover my devices."

219. Alexa would scan to see devices that are within range and then attempt to discover them. Shortly, you are alerted about which device Alexa has discovered.

220. To see and customize your smart devices, tap **Devices** in the Alexa app.

Linking Your Devices to Alexa Using Guided Discovery

221. To link a smart home device that is not ZigBee-supported (e.g., TP-Link) but WiFi enabled, power the device and launch the Alexa mobile application and from the home page, tap **Devices** then the plus icon, and finally **Add Device**. Select your smart home device as well as the brand of the device. Follow the onscreen guide to complete the process.

Linking Your Devices to Alexa Using Smart Home Skills

222. A third-party skill or a companion application for your device serves as the enabler for the smart device with Alexa. In other words, when enabled, you can easily link your smart device that associates with it with Alexa. Every smart device, especially those not manufactured by Amazon, comes with an enabler app otherwise referred to as **skill**.

223. To link up your device with Alexa using a skill, power on the smart device and in the Alexa app, go to **Menu** ▤ then **Skills**. Touch the search 🔍 icon and type the skill name for your device then conduct a search for it. From the search result, tap the skill for your device and **Enable** it. **Sign In** to your account with them if necessary and follow the instruction shown on the screen to complete the process. You can also move from **Skills > Categories > Smart Home** and then search for relevant Skill. Alternatively, search and enable relevant Skills on Amazon.com.

224. Next, download the device app from manufacturer's website, Play- or App- Store and set up the smart device following the instructions coming from the app. Make sure the smart device app is connected through the same WiFi network with your Echo Studio.

225. To connect your device, from the Alexa app, go to **Menu,** ▤ and select **Add Device.** Under **All Devices**, select the nature of your device and then your **device's brand**. If necessary, sign into your smart device companion app and then go back to the Alexa app and tap **Continue**.

226. Finally, your smart device is ready and registered under **Devices** in Alexa app. If your device is not added to the Alexa app, ask Alexa to discover it ("Alexa, discover devices"). Adding any other smart home device follow similar process.

227. Take note that once your smart home device is set up with the Amazon Alexa using the required skill for the device, anyone with the right command can trigger the smart device to work. Hence, it is recommended that you put off the microphones on your

Echo device when leaving the house as well as setting up a PIN code on your smartphone that holds the Alexa app to prevent authorized access to Alexa through your mobile phone.

Pairing Multiple Echo Smart Speakers for Stereo Sound

228. In your Alexa app, tap **Devices** 🏠 on the home page. Tap the **plus** ⊕ icon at the upper right corner. Select **Add Stereo Pair**. Select your devices to pair them. Tap **Next** at the upper right corner of the screen and follow the onscreen prompts to complete the process.

229. Note that all speakers must be connected to the same WiFi network and they must be online.

Troubleshooting Smart Home Connections

230. Ensure that your smart devices are recommended by Amazon or compatible with Alexa.

231. Make sure that required smart device Skills have been enabled.

232. Make sure that you've downloaded and configured smart device companion application.

233. Make sure that **all** your connections are on the same WiFi network.

234. Make sure that all your smart devices and Alexa are working on updated mobile app.

235. Don't forget to Philips Hue Bridge button when trying to discover it in the Alexa app.

Other times,

236. You may have to restart your smart home and Alexa-enabled devices.

237. Forget or unlink a smart device and then disable associated Skill in the Alexa app and try reconnecting it again.

238. It is strongly recommended that you set up a personal WiFi network to power your smart home.

Setting Up Music Services

239. In the Alexa app homepage, tap the **Music & Books** icon. Scroll down and tap **More Music Streaming Services** to setup your music services on your Echo device. Select your favorite **Music Provider** from the dropdown and link your account with them. To **disconnect** from a Music Service, select **Unlink account from Alexa** against the music service you want to disconnect.

Useful commands for music

240. Basic controls: "Alexa, [shuffle / stop shuffle / stop / pause / play / resume]."

241. Going a little advanced: "Alexa, play latest track by <artist name>," "Alexa, play songs similar to 70s."

242. Music services: "Alexa, play [artist name / song title / album title], or "Alexa, play <radio station name> on <Music Service>," or "Alexa, play <playlist name>."

243. Even more: "Alexa, play Prime Playlist," or "Alexa, play <song title> from <Music Service>."

244. To create a playlist: "Alexa, create a playlist."

245. To play from a playlist: "Alexa, play playlist Country Christmas."

246. To add songs to a playlist: "Alexa, add [song / artist name / album] to <playlist name>."

247. **Tip:** If you are not comfortable with explicit songs, in the Alexa app, navigate: **Settings > Music > Explicit Filter**. Toggle **Explicit Filter On**. Using voice, you can say, "Alexa, block explicit music" to turn it on or "Alexa, stop blocking explicit music" to turn it off.

248. **Tip:** Where you are unable to launch some Music Services due to explicit filtering, please turn off the feature and try again.

My Music Library / Amazon Music

249. To set up your Amazon Music Service, launch your Alexa app and tap the **Music & Book** icon then select **Music**. See all Music Services listed under **Music**. Select **Amazon Music**.

250. On the **Playlist** tab, you can choose from **Decade, Artist, Genres or Mood & Activities** then a **Category**. Finally, choose a **Playlist** to play. Control your playback as desired.

251. Take advantage of the search field to find songs or albums quickly. The tabs— Playlist, Artists, Albums, and Songs are also straightforward. They help classified your music. To request for music stored in your Music Library, say, "Alexa, play [playlist, artists, albums, or song name] from [Amazon Prime Music / My Music Library]. Example, "Alexa, play Chris Brown from Amazon Prime Music."

Amazon Music: Prime and Unlimited

Amazon Prime

252. After **My Amazon Music**, you get to **Amazon Prime Music**. Here, you can access a collection of Amazon music. Your Music Library houses your music purchases and Playlists from Amazon based on your subscriptions. Using a computer, visit alexa.amazon.com and click on Music, Video and Books. Scroll down to **Music** section. From there, you can click on **My Music Library** or **Prime Music**.

253. **Tip:** Download the <u>Amazon Music application</u> for your computer and log into your account to easily access your Amazon music from your computer.

254. With your Prime Music Subscription and in your Alexa app, tap **Music & Book** and browse through your music in the two categories—Stations and Playlists. While the Stations category is based on either an era of music, artist, or genre, the Playlists category is curated by the Amazon. Here, you can select music tracks but in Stations, you can't. You may need to walk around to familiarize yourself with the Playlist names so that you can easily request from Alexa. The format is simple: "Alexa, play [name of playlist] from Amazon Prime Music."

255. To add a Prime Music Playlist to your music library, visit **<u>Amazon Prime Music</u>** using your computer and then browse through available **Playlists** (see link at upper left under **Browse**). Hover a Playlist and then click the plus sign ⊞ to add it to your music library. Click on the more options ⋮ icon

for options to share, follow, go to playlist, play next, or add the playlist to queue.

256. Alternatively, in the Alexa app, navigate tap the **Music, Video & Books** icon, and then tap **Prime Music** and finally **Playlists**. Search for a preferred playlist and start playing it. From there, you can tell Alexa to add it to your library. The playlist is subsequently listed in your music library pages.

257. It's not straightforward to add an album to your music library. We will try to play around it. Again, visit Amazon Prime Music on your computer. For example, search for a song title e.g., "Drunk by Ed Sheeran." Under **Prime Songs**, click the **more options** ⋮ icon and then click **View Album**. From here, click the plus sign ⊕ to add the album to your music library. This is just a simple way of how to go about this. From here, you can say, "Alexa, play [album name by artist name] from my music library."

258. **Amazon music subscriptions:** You must have a subscription with Amazon— Amazon Prime or Amazon Music Unlimited or both. The Prime Music standard annual subscription is $119, while the standard monthly subscription is $12.99 – all with a 30-day free trial. Students can also enjoy a $6.49 and $59 monthly and annual subscription respectively.

Amazon Music Unlimited

259. If you can't afford the Amazon Prime Music plan, you can opt for the Amazon Music Unlimited plan with a monthly subscription of $7.99 for individuals and $14.99 for a family (up to 6 members permitted). You can also go for an annual subscription on any of these plans. If you own the Echo Show, Amazon Tap, Echo Look, Echo, Echo Dot, or Fire TV, you can subscribe to a monthly plan of $3.99 ($4.99 for students). Note that this plan works only for one of the devices listed here.

Tidal

To get started, create your Tidal account on tidal.com. On your Alexa app, tap **Music & Books** and then **Browse Music**. Scroll down and tap **Tidal**. Enable the Tidal music skill by tapping **Enable to Use**. Connect your Tidal account and you are done. Alternatively, say, "Alexa, open Tidal." to enable the Tidal music skill. From here, you can request for a specific playlist, song by name or favorite artist. Format: "Alexa, play [playlist / song name] on Tidal."

iHeartRadio

260. To setup your iHeartRadio on Alexa, sign up on **iheart.com** using a Computer, and sign in with same login details on Alexa app via **Settings > Music & Books > Music > iHeartRadio**.

261. You can listen to over 850+ stations on iHeartRadio on your Echo Show. Content includes talk, music, news, sports, etc. Well, you should have your favorite station in mind

but if you don't, head over to **iheart.com** and look at some channels there. You can choose to search by location or genre.

262. To play any channel of your choice, use the format: "Alexa, play <radio station's name> on iHeartRadio." Example, "Alexa, play Kiss FM on iHeartRadio," or "Alexa, play Kiss FM on iHeartRadio on Group 1" where Group 1 is your Echo speaker group name for a Multi-Room Music setup. To stop playing, say, "Alexa, stop."

Spotify

263. Like the iHeartRadio, use your PC to create an account with Spotify then come back to Alexa app and log in to the music service with your login details via **Setting > Music & Books > Music > Spotify**.

264. If you are on Spotify Premium, you can use the Spotify app on your smartphone or tablet device as a remote. This means you should have a **Spotify Connect** subscription.

265. From here, you can say, "Alexa, Connect to Spotify" to enable your Spotify Connect subscription or "Alexa, play <genre> on Spotify."

Pandora

266. Sign up on **pandora.com** using a Computer and on the Alexa app, go to **Settings > Music & Books > Music > Pandora > Enable**. Sign in with your Pandora account information.

267. To request a song: "Alexa, play <artist name> radio from Pandora." Where the song isn't available, a station would be created for you.

268. To vote a song: "Alexa give a [Thumb Up / Thumb Down] to this song."

269. To control playback: "Alexa, [play / stop] music on Pandora."

270. To skip a song: "Alexa, skip this song."

271. To control volume: "Alexa, turn volume [down / up]."

272. To know what's playing: "Alexa, what's playing?"

273. Pandora Premium users can request a playlist, specific song or album to be played for them, e.g., "Alexa, play One Dance by Drake on Pandora."

274. To disable Pandora on Alexa

275. On the Alexa app, go to Settings > Music & Books > Music > Pandora > Disable.

SiriusXM

276. Follow a similar method like the above to **Enable** SiriusXM on Alexa. Once enabled, **Link your Account** with your login details. To learn more, go to **siriusxm.com**.

TuneIn

277. In the Alexa app, tap on the **Menu** icon then Skills. Use the search bar to search for and **Enable** TuneIn Live Skill. To use your

voice to enable TuneIn, say, "Alexa, open TuneIn Live" and say "Yes" to her prompt.

278. You can stream news, music, sport and podcasts from TuneIn. TuneIn works with content providers such as NHL, MLB, NBA, NFL, Al Jazeera, MSNBC, CNBC, Newsy, etc.

Deezer

279. Deezer is a premium music service on Alexa. You can listen to Deezer using an Alexa-enabled device in the US, UK, Canada, Germany, Ireland, New Zealand, and Australia. Sign up for a paid account on **deezer.com.**

280. Deezer is already listed on Alexa and all you need to do is to activate and start using it. To get started, tap on **Music & Books** icon from the Alexa homepage and select **Deezer** and subsequently tap **Enable** to initiate the activation process. Enter your login details to fully activate it on Alexa.

Apple Music

281. From the Alexa app, go to Skills, search and enable the Apple Music skill. Connect your Apple ID and start using it.

282. Alternatively, in the Alexa app, tap **Menu > Settings > Alexa Preferences > Music > Link New Service > Apple Music > Enable to Use**. From here, sign in using your Apple ID. Request Alexa to play from your Apple music: songs, artist, playlists, etc. "...on Apple Music"—if Apple Music isn't your default music service.

Setting Your Default Music Service

283. A default Music Service attends to your music request any time you need it. When your default Music Service is set, you can simply call for music without necessarily specifying what service should fulfill the request. A request such as, "Alexa, play music" is going to be handled by your default Music Service. Here, you don't specify where the music should come from (e.g., *"Alexa, play Ignition by R. Kelly* ~~on Pandora~~), so Alexa

simply starts playing from your default Music Service.

284. You can **Select Your Default Music Service** from **Menu > Settings > Music > Account Settings > Default Services** in the Alexa app.

Multi-Room Music with the ES5

285. To get started, connect your Amazon Echo speakers on the same network. Apart from having your Echo speakers all connected to the same WiFi connection, you'll also need at best an Amazon Music Unlimited or a Prime Music Account. While you can setup a Multi-Room Music with a Prime Music account, an Amazon Music Unlimited account is nevertheless the best for this.

286. A Multi-Room Music setup with a **Prime Music account** can only enable you to stream a music channel (e.g., Pandora only) at a time to a speaker group, while a **Music Unlimited with a Family Plan** can stream multi-music channels (e.g., iHeartRadio and

SiriusXM) at the same time to different speaker groups. However, take note that Multi-Room Music setup does not work with speakers connected over Bluetooth.

287. To get started with **Multi-Room Music** setup, click on **Devices** from the homepage to see controls for smart home devices. Tap the plus sign , and then **Add Multi-Room Music Speakers.** Name your group either by choosing from system suggestions or inputting your custom name. Select the Echo speakers you want to use in forming a group. Once done, tap **Save**.

288. **Tips:** Note that a speaker can't be added to two or more groups. You can always remove your Echo speaker from **its group** under **Speaker Groups** in **Devices**.

289. Once setup is completed for the group, it's ready for use. Simply say, "Alexa, play music on 'Group 1." Here, Alexa plays from the default music service. You can also say, "Alexa, play SiriusXM on 'Group 1" where 'Group 1' is the Echo speaker group name. You can stop the playback from any Echo.

290. **More useful invocations:** "Alexa, play [artist/playlist name] on [Echo speaker group name]" or "Alexa, play [name of radio station] on Pandora on [Echo speaker group name]."

291. To control which speaker within a group plays what, use the format: "Alexa, play TuneIn on 'Group one' and play SiriusXM on 'Group two'" where 'Group one' and 'Group two' are Echo speaker group names where your default music service is set to Amazon Music Unlimited.

Watching Video on Your ES5

Even with a little screen, you can still enjoy watching video on the ES5. With a resolution of 960 x 480, the picture quality is just fine.

292. To get started with video on the ES5, swipe from right, and then tap **Video**. From here, you can watch your prime movies, TV Shows or contents from your library.

293. You can fast forward or rewind by 10 seconds.

294. To see closed captions, tap the button on the top right corner of the screen. From here, you can set the **Audio** language that you want to hear and turn ON / OFF the **Subtitle**.

295. You can also set the video to full screen by tapping the button just beside that of closed caption.

296. Tap on the screen to see the Pause / Play button.

297. With supported Video Providers, you can watch even more videos on your ES5. If your ES5 is also connected to a Fire TV, you must specify where you want the request to be fulfilled by saying, "…on <Echo device name>" after your request, e.g., "Alexa, show me **'Homecoming'** on <Echo device name>." This way, your request is directed to your Echo screen and not your Fire TV.

Some useful invocation about movies

298. To find out number of theaters showing what movie at what time, you can say, "Alexa, which theater is [playing / showing] **'Homecoming'** tonight?"

299. To see a movie starring your favorite actor or actress: "Alexa, play a movie starring <actor/actress name>."

300. To know the closest movie times: "Alexa, show me the closest movie times."

301. To see more results, "Alexa, show more."

302. To get movie information: "Alexa, is **'Homecoming'** any good?"

303. To get information about a movie director or release date: "Alexa, who directed the **'Homecoming'**?"

304. Find out a movie released date: "Alexa, when was **'Homecoming'** movie released?"

Streaming YouTube

305. The Amazon Echo Show uses the Silk or Firefox Browser to stream YouTube videos. Say, "Alexa, open [Silk / Firefox]" to launch any of the two Browsers. Sadly, you can't parse a voice command to open YouTube while you are already on the browser interface but you can say, "Alexa, open YouTube" and YouTube would be launch on your default browser. Once on the browser page, you'll have to type YouTube URL (youtube.com) manually to access it and thereafter bookmark it for ease of access in subsequent times. This will continue until Amazon finds a way of getting the YouTube app on the ES5 and until then, you'll have to access it through the browser. We hope future updates would fix this.

Watching TV Shows, Movies and Business News from CNBC, Hulu, and NBC

Open an account with these providers (where necessary) using a PC and then login with your details in the Alexa mobile app via

Settings > TV & Video. At **TV & Video**, select your preferred content provider and setup your service.

Once your setup with any of these channels is completed, you can request for TV Shows or channels using your voice. You might need a subscription to enjoy premium service.

Hulu

To begin, subscribe to a content plan on hulu.com. Hulu is particularly interesting because they also link up with other providers such as NBC, HGTV, ABC, Disney channel, etc. To get started, say, "Alexa, open Hulu."

Tip: If you own a FireTV, there's no point subscribing to Hulu since it's included in FireTV.

306. To get started, say, "Alexa, open Hulu."

307. "Alexa, ask Hulu to tune to ESPN."

308. "Alexa, ask Hulu to play Seinfeld."

309. "Alexa, show me channels on Hulu."

310. "Alexa, rewind."

311. "Alexa, play next episode."

312. "Alexa, play episodes of [programming]."

313. "Alexa, change channel to [programming]."

314. **Tip:** To watch live content, get a Live TV plan on Hulu and link up to it from the Alexa app via **Devices > Settings > TV & Videos > Hulu > Link Your Alexa Device**.

CNBC

315. For CNBC, get started by enabling the CNBC skill using your voice, "Alexa, enable CNBC."

316. **Tip:** To watch live content, get a Live TV plan on Hulu and link up to it from the Alexa app via **Devices > Settings > TV & Videos > Hulu > Link Your Alexa Device** to select your Provider. You can subscribe to CNBC Pro for premium content.

Useful voice commands

317. "Alexa, [show / watch] the Cramer Remix."

318. "Alexa, [play / stream / watch / find / search / search for / show me / open / turn on / tune to] <Video content name> (e.g., Cartoon Network, Channels, Networks, Sci-Fi shows, Movies, Movies with…, Episodes of…, Sports, etc.) on [Hulu / NBC]"

319. Get the news on CNBC: "Alexa, ask CNBC for latest news."

320. Get quotes: "Alexa, ask CNBC for pricing info for [stocks / ETFs / futures / indices]."

321. Get US Market Information on S&P 500, NASDAQ, and the Dow: "Alexa, ask CNBC, what's happening with the US markets?"

General controls during playback

322. To see sub-title: "Alexa, turn [off / on] captions."

323. "Alexa, [play / stop / pause / rewind / fast forward]."

324. **Tip:** The video fast forward or rewinds by 10 seconds.

325. "Alexa, [go forward / go backward] by '60' [seconds / minutes]."

326. "Alexa, [restart / play next / next episode / skip back / volume up / volume down]."

327. "Alexa, [switch channel to / change channel to] on CNBC / NBC]."

NBC

Catch up with great shows on NBC. Enable the NBC skill to get started by saying, "Alexa, open NBC."

328. "Alexa, show **'Bring the funny'** on NBC."

329. "Alexa, show **'New Amsterdam'** on NBC."

330. "Alexa, pause."

331. "Alexa, fast forward three minutes."

332. "Alexa, search for **'comedies'** on NBC."

Watching Movies Trailers from IMDB

333. Catch a glimpse of your trailers from IMDB using the Echo device with a voice command. It's simple, you can say, "Alexa, show the trailer of the movie <movie name>."

Watching from your Amazon Video & Prime Video Library and Amazon Channels Subscriptions

334. You can also watch TV Shows and Movies from your Amazon Prime Video Library or play programming from Amazon Channels subscriptions through your browser

or smart Amazon devices with a screen such as the Fire TV, TV, Echo Spot and Show, or on your Android and iOS devices.

Amazon Video

335. Search through **Movies, Music & Games** on **amazon.com** with your ES5's browser to buy or rent Amazon Video. You can also access these titles with your Prime Membership.

Tip: Any time you rent or buy a title from Amazon, find it in your Video Library.

Prime Video

336. With your Prime Membership, you can browse through thousands of content: movies and TV shows at no extra cost to you. Most times, membership for the first month is free and after that you can go for annual subscription (over $119 per year), simple Prime Video ($8.99 per month) or full Prime Monthly ($12.99 per month). Learn more about these subscriptions on **amazon.com.**

Amazon Channels Subscription

337. Channel subscription offers content from 3rd party Video Services such as Showtime, PBS Kids, HBO, etc. To access content from these providers, you'll need to be on Prime Membership all-inclusive subscription. However, that's on one part, the other part is that these additional contents not offered by Amazon are charged separately. While ShowTime's subscription is $10.99 per month, HBO cost $14.99 per month). To learn more, go to Prime Video and then Prime Video Channels on **amazon.com.**

338. To search your library using Alexa, say, "Alexa, show my video library" or "Alexa, show my Watch List." From the search result displayed on your screen, you can scroll and tap on your preferred title.

339. To search a specific title: "Alexa, show me <movie/content title>" or "Alexa, find <TV series name>."

340. To search by genre or actor, say, "Alexa, show <genre> movies" or "Alexa, show me <name of actor> movies."

Watching Free TV Stations

341. You can watch many international free TV stations on your Echo screen. It's simple and straight to the point: the skill to enable in this regard is Stream Player. As usual, to enable, say, "Alexa, enable Stream Player." From here, you can call a channel by name or number, e.g., "Alexa, tell Stream Player to [play / show / launch] <channel name>," "Alexa, tell Stream Player to [play / show / launch] <channel number."

Watch Unlimited Music Video on Vevo

342. With Vevo, you can watch unlimited music video for free on your Echo device with a screen.

343. To enable the Vevo skill, say, "Alexa, enable Vevo."

Some useful voice commands

344. "Alexa, play some music videos on Vevo."

345. By artist name: "Alexa, ask Vevo to play <artist name> music videos."

346. By song title: "Alexa, ask Vevo to play <song title> music videos."

347. By genre: "Alexa, ask Vevo to play <genre> music videos."

348. By popular demand: "Alexa, ask Vevo to play music videos"

349. **Tip:** Use basic control voice commands to control playback.

Connecting Your FireTV

350. To set up your FireTV, from the Alexa app, tap **Devices > Menu > Settings > TV & Videos > FireTV > Manage Devices > Link Another Device > <Your FireTV> >**

Continue. From here, select the Echo device that's going to control your FireTV and then tap **Link Devices**. You're done!

351. **Tips:** (1) Feel free to link more than an Echo device to the FireTV but control it with one device at a time. (2) Your Alexa app, Echo device and FireTV must be registered or linked with same Amazon account. (3) Alexa can play content from apps installed on your TV and Prime Video.

352. To a play TV show or movie, "Alexa, watch [show / movie] title on FireTV"

353. To play TV show or movie on FireTV app, "Alexa, play [show / movie] title on [app name] on FireTV."

354. To play a genre, "Alexa, play [movie genre] on FireTV."

355. To play a genre on FireTV app, "Alexa, play [movie genre] on [app name] on FireTV."

356. To search for movies and TV shows, including Prime Video and supported apps,

"Alexa, find TV shows and movies on FireTV."

357. To search for a movie title or genre, "Alexa, search for [title / genre] on FireTV."

358. To see movie titles with actors, "Alexa, show movie titles with [actor's name] on FireTV."

359. To search for content within your installed apps, "Alexa, search within apps, "Alexa, find [TV show / movie] on [app name] on FireTV."

360. "Alexa, search for [genre / title] on [app name] on FireTV."

361. To see TV shows or movies on FireTV app, "Alexa, show me [TV shows / movies] on [app name] on FireTV."

Control playback

362. "Alexa [play / pause / stop / resume / rewind [timeframe in seconds or minutes]."

363. "Alexa, fast-forward by [timeframe]."

364. "Alexa, rewind [timeframe]."

365. "Alexa, [next / next episode]."

366. "Alexa, show from beginning."

367. "Alexa, go to [network / channel] on [app name]."

368. "Alexa, show [channel / network] on FireTV."

Alexa Routines with the ES5

Alexa can perform multiple actions with just a single voice command through a routine. For example, you can say, "Alexa, I'm stepping out" to have her switch the lights and plugs off, or maybe saying, "Alexa, what's in the news?" to have her play your flash briefings.

Alexa routines can automate how your Echo device works with other smart home devices. A command is sent to Alexa and that follows your Smart Device being triggered for action. For example, you can set "Alexa, good night" to turn off your smart light bulbs. Alexa routines can work on a range of Amazon Echo devices including but not limited to Amazon Echo, Echo Plus, Echo Show, and Echo Dot.

Alexa routines can stop audio or play it for minutes, make announcements, send notifications or trigger a Do-Not-Disturb for a time.

369. To get started with Alexa routine, launch the Alexa app, tap on the **Menu** then select **Routines**. Create a routine by tapping the plus ⊕ icon at the top right side of the screen.

370. Next, create a trigger by selecting **When This Happens.** You can either create a routine when you say a phrase using your **Voice**, at **Schedule** time, when arriving or leaving the house, when an Echo device does something,

or when you press the Echo Button. We'll demonstrate with using your voice, and at schedule time as well as on how to add a smart device or set music to play in a routine.

371. Note that the routines you've created are listed under the **Your Routines** tab. Tap **Featured** to see some featured routines that you can try.

Creating a Routine with a Phrase (Voice)

372. If selecting the first option, enter a phrase, e.g., "Alexa, good morning" and tap **Save**. Next, **Add Action** under **Alexa Will** to work with the phrase you've just set. We have actions such as news, traffic, smart home, weather, calendar, Alexa says, messaging, music, and more. Simply think of something logical and set a routine for it. For instance, if you select **News** [and then **Add**]. Finally, tap **Save**. From the setup, Alexa would deliver to you what's in the news fetching from your flash briefings. As a result, every time you say, "Alexa, good morning," the next thing you will get is news from your flash briefing channels.

373. If you select **Alexa Says**, there are still many options. Alexa can sing a song for you, tell a joke, tell a story, and more. For every option you pick, tap on **Add** to register it. Again, this means that every time you say, "Alexa, good morning," what you will get is Alexa singing a song for you, telling you a joke, telling you a story, etc. This is just how Alexa routine works. Interesting right?

374. **Tips:** Under **Alexa Will**, (1) You can add more than a single action, (2) You can add a custom action, (3) You can also delete an action by tapping the minus button. (4) Under **From**, select the Echo device you want to execute your routine.

How to disable a routine

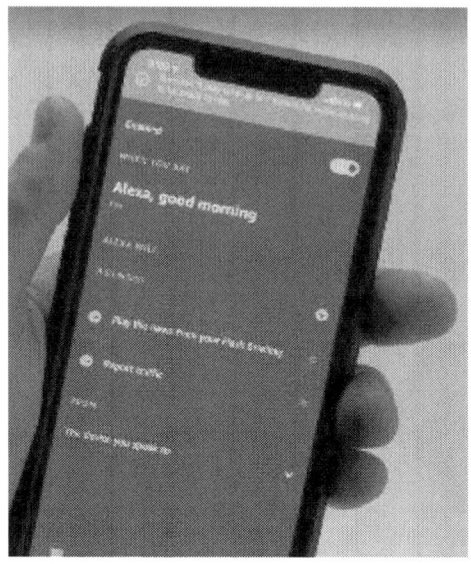

375. Under **Your Routines** tab in the Routines home screen, tap on the routine you want to disable and then toggle it OFF (the slider goes left).

Creating a Routine at Scheduled Time and Day

376. If going for **Schedule**, choose the **time** you'll like your routine to be activated [and then tap **Done**] and also choose when you want it to repeat. You may decide to choose every day, weekdays (Monday to Friday), weekend (Saturday and Sunday), or any particular day. Confirm your selection and tap **Done**.

377. Next, add an action against the time and day(s) you want your routine to occur by tapping **Add Action**. Such an action can be getting weather information, news, playing music, traffic, smart home, etc. and you are **Done**. Finally, tap **Save** when you are through with your selection.

Adding Smart Home Devices to Routine

378. Under **Alexa Will**, tap **Add Action** and choose **Smart Home**. From the two options, tap **Control Device**. Next, select your preferred device, e.g., bulb, plug, etc. You can continue adding more smart devices and selecting what you want happen to the device when scheduled time and day is reached. Finally, tap **Save**.

379. **Tip:** You can create a routine to turn them ON and another routine to turn them OFF.

Adding Music to a Routine

380.   It's rather easy to create a routine with your favorite music. A music routine can pass for an alarm if you create it using scheduled time and day. To get started, from the Alexa app, add a music action (Add Action) for the condition that you want your routine to occur by tapping on the plus (+) icon. On the next screen, pick a song by typing in the song title. Next, select the **Music Provider**. Your music could come from your music library, Pandora, Amazon, Spotify, TuneIn or iHeartRadio. Tap **Save** to continue.

Having Alexa Say Something in a Routine

381.   Alexa can say a phrase when a routine is triggered. Such phrases could be a welcome home message, a compliment, a goodbye, good night or good morning message, a birthday wish, etc.

382.   To get started, under **Alexa Will**, tap to **Add Action** and select **Alexa Says**. You can type a Custom phrase or pick from the list. You can also tap on **Phrases** from the list to

see more. Follow through and select your preferred phrase and then tap **Add**. Finally, **Save**.

Linking Your Calendar

383. Alexa supports Apple (Calendar only), Google (Email and Calendar), Microsoft (Email and Calendar) and Microsoft Exchange (Calendar only) through Office 365 and Outlook. To make it happen, on the Alexa app, go to **Settings,** scroll down and tap on **Email & Calendar**. Select your preferred service and **Connect your Account** supplying your login credentials (if necessary). Grant Alexa necessary permissions and finally, your account email and calendar are added.

384. To keep things easy, work with just a Calendar. Tap on the checkbox against the calendar that you've setup earlier then go **Back** (see arrow at top left). Continue to configure your chosen calendar for Alexa in **Email & Calendar**. Finally, you are set. Remember that household members can also access your Email and Calendar.

385. At this point, you can add events to your calendar using the format: "Alexa, add <event name> to my calendar by <time> on <when>." Example, "Alexa, add meeting to my calendar by 2pm tomorrow," or "Alexa, add travel to my calendar by 5am on Monday."

How to join a conference call

386. Putting in place or setting up a conferencing solution such as Amazon Chime, Skype, Zoom, or Cisco WebEx set up, and also linking your calendar such as Google G-Suite or Gmail, Apple iCloud, Outlook, or Microsoft Office 365 to the Alexa application, you can join a conference call with others. Set your calendar in the Alexa app via, **Menu > Settings > Calendar & Email**.

387. To get started with a conferencing, say, "Alexa, join my meeting" or "Alexa, join my *'Board meeting'*," where 'Board meeting' is the name of your meeting as marked on your connected calendar.

388. While the conference call is still going on, you can say, "Alexa, hang up" to end the call, or "Alexa, press 5" to enter touch tones. Remember, you must have added the meeting to your calendar before this time.

389. Running late for a meeting? Let the attendees know about it. Say, "Alexa, I am running [#] minutes late." "Running late for *'Board meeting'*?" Echo asks. You then reply: "Yes." Echo then send an email to the attendees with the message, "I am running [#] minutes late."

390. You want to go late to the next meeting? Say, "Alexa, I will be [#] minutes late for my next meeting."

391. To schedule a 1:1 meeting with a co-worker, say, "Alexa, schedule a meeting with *Garten*" to get started.

392. To reschedule a meeting, say, "Alexa, move / reschedule my *'Board meeting'* to [time] e.g. 6 PM tomorrow or on *'Thursday'*"

Alarms, Reminders and Timers

You can use a voice command to cancel or set countdown timers and manage settings in the Alexa app. It could be a named or countdown timer — as you wish. You can also set your alarms and reminders using your voice or the Alexa app.

How to set a Timer

393. A named timer could sound like: "Alexa, set a **sleep timer** for 90 minutes," "Alexa, set a **lunch timer** for 30 minutes."

394. You can also set **multiple** timers by saying, "Alexa, set a **second timer** for 10 minutes."

395. You want to check timer status? "Alexa, what are my timers?" or "Alexa, what time is left on the lunch timer?"

396. A **countdown** timer could sound like: "Alexa, stop playing in 50 minutes" or "Alexa, set a timer for 20 minutes."

397. While your timer is running, you can say, "Alexa, [cancel / stop] sleep timer," "Alexa, what time is remaining in sleep timer?" or "Alexa, what time is remaining in my timer?"

398. To cancel a timer, say, "Alexa, cancel the **lunch timer**" or "Alexa, cancel the 20-minute timer."

How to set a Reminder

399. "Alexa, add a reminder about <name of activity> by <time> tomorrow" e.g., "Alexa, add a reminder about going to church by 6:00 AM tomorrow."

How to set an Alarm

400. To set an alarm for any particular **time**, say, "Alexa, set an alarm for 4 AM," "Alexa, wake me up by 4 AM in the morning."

401. If you want to rather set a **music alarm**, you can say, "Alexa, wake me up to [artist name / song title / genre / playlist name / album] at 4 a.m.," or "Alexa, wake me up to Urban FM at 4 AM on TuneIn."

402. Setting an alarm on **repeat mode**, you can say, "Alexa, set a repeating alarm for weekdays at 4 AM."

403. To setup your Reminders, Alarms or Timers manually, go to **Reminders & Alarms** under **Menu** in the Alexa app.

Weather and Traffic

404. In the Alexa app, set your traffic preference to get traffic information within your location. Go to **Settings > Alexa Preferences > Traffic**. Enter your starting and destination addresses then **Save Changes**.

405. To ask for traffic information, say: "Alexa, how's traffic?" "Alexa, how is the traffic right now?" "Alexa, what is my commute?"

406. For information on weather in your location, you can say, "Alexa, what's the weather?" or "Alexa, will it rain today?" "Alexa, how is the weather this weekend? "Alexa, show me the weather forecast."

Teaching Alexa to Always Recognize Your Voice

Voice training can be done by setting up a Voice or User Profile. The essence of doing this is to enable Alexa understands you better and interact with you closely — as you! You can refer to this as customized interactions.

407. To get started, launch the Alexa app, tap the **Menu** ≡ icon and go to **Settings**, **Accounts** and finally tap on **Your Voice**. **Begin** the process of making Alexa learn your voice. You can also initiate this process with a

voice command: "Alexa, [learn / train] my voice."

408. If using the mobile app to create a voice profile, tapping the **drop-down** menu would show devices that you have. Select a device and start the process. Right now, it is important that you turn off the microphones ("Alexa, turn off microphones on <Echo dot device name>") of other Echo devices in the house (if any) while you concentrate with the selected one. Since this process is conducted using the Alexa app, you may not necessarily need to repeat it with other Echo devices you might have in your house. They'll automatically pick up.

409. Once the process is initiated, Alexa would lead you through the training with voice prompts. Say them out loud with your natural voice, and from a position you may sit or stand to send requests. Don't go too close to your Echo device. Again, try to reduce background noise as much as possible and keep your Echo device away from walls (say 10 inches away). If you miss a prompt and Alexa doesn't get it right, **Try Again**. **Complete** the process when you get to the end.

410. At this point, you can connect your voice profile to your **Amazon Music Unlimited** account. Continue to use the device when the process is completed and try to check if Alexa can recognize your voice after 30 minutes by asking her who you are ("Alexa, who am I?").

411. If you have any issue, reach out to Amazon via **Help & Feedback**. Select the concerned device and log your complaint.

412. To create more voice profiles with the same Echo, new users must download the Alexa app into their mobile phones and login to Amazon account that hosts the Echo device and then initiate the process from their Alexa mobile app. Again, the essence of this is to have a personalized experience with Alexa such as news briefings, making calls and messaging from contact lists, etc.

413. Always ask Alexa who you are before sending requests to her to be sure she's listening and processing commands from and for the right person. If she's wrong on who's

talking, tell her to stop or cancel so that you don't access another person's content. As you keep using Alexa, it masters your voice even more.

How to delete a voice profile

414. In the Alexa app, go to **Settings > Alexa Account > Recognized Voices > Your Voice > Delete my Voice.**

415. **Tip:** Deleting a Voice Profile means that you'll no longer enjoy a personalized experience with Alexa.

Shop Amazon Securely with Alexa

416. Shopping with Alexa using the Amazon Echo Show takes a brand new level. Fortunately and unfortunately, you'll have to be on Amazon Prime to be able to shop using Alexa. To get started, use the format: *"Alexa, buy <product name>,"* e.g. *"Alexa, order Amazon Echo Dot 3rd Generation Black color."* From here, Alexa searches through Amazon store

and displays search results. To order the first, you can say, *"Alexa, buy this,"* or *"Alexa, show more."*

417. To begin, sign up for Amazon Prime and enable your 1-Click Ordering.

Setting up confirmation code for your shopping

418. A confirmation code is needed when you've added a product to your cart but not paying for them right away. To set up a code, go to **Menu** ▤, **Settings, Alexa Account** on your Alexa app and select **Voice Purchasing.** Set your 4-digit code. With this code, after adding some items to your cart, Alexa would ask if you are ordering them immediately where your 4-digit code would be required to complete the transaction.

419. You may not need a confirmation code to complete a purchase if you are searching for and buying the product immediately without necessarily adding it to the cart. For example, you can say, "Alexa, order Amazon Echo Show 5 black color from Amazon." Alexa would now search for the product and

return with a reply: "Great, I found Amazon Echo Show 5, it's $89.9, should I place an order for it?" Then you can say, "Go ahead" or "Yes" and your order is placed.

Ordering more than an item of same product or each of different items

420. If you want to order **more than a piece of an item**; that would work but if you want to buy **different items at the same time** or **as a single order**, that won't work. So you can say, *"Alexa, order 5 pieces of black Amazon Echo Input"* and not something like, *"Alexa, order 2 black Amazon Echo Input and 1 black Amazon Echo Dot 2nd generation."* Voice shopping for different items are done separately or you can add everything to cart and place order with your confirmation code.

Some invocation phrases for shopping

421. Do you want to re-order essentials from Amazon? "Alexa, buy more deodorant," or "Alexa, re-order deodorant."

422. You want to track your packages from Amazon? "Alexa, track my order" or "Alexa, where's my stuff?"

423. You want to order an Alexa device? "Alexa, order an [Alexa device name],"

424. You want to build your cart? e.g., "Alexa, add a mouse to my cart."

425. You want to order Lyft for a ride? "Alexa, ask Lyft for a ride," where Lyft is a skill by the Lyft company operating cab services. That means you must first of all enable it.

426. You feel like buying a nice song while listening to it on Amazon Music? "Alexa, buy this song," or "Alexa, buy this album."

427. Or finding a new music to buy? "Alexa, shop for new music by [artist name]."

Do you want to buy a song / album from a known artist? "Alexa, buy [song / album] by [artist name]."

428.   You want to know about today's deals? "Alexa, what are your deals?" or "Alexa, what deals do you have?"

429.   **Tip:** Again, it's great to set up a **passcode** to prevent someone else sending a voice command to Alexa to make purchases without your consent. To begin, navigate, **Settings > Alexa Account > Voice Purchasing.**

Buy from Whole Foods Market on Amazon Prime Now

430.   "Alexa, what Whole Foods deals do you have today?"

431.   "Alexa, add [product / item name] to my Whole Foods cart."

Creating and Managing Your Shopping / To-do list

Amazon list comes with two default lists: Shopping and To-do. You can easily start adding items to these lists through your Alexa app or using your voice. You can also create custom lists and add items to them.

432. To create a custom list using the Alexa app, tap on the **Menu** ☰ icon and select **Lists**. Select **Create List** and type in a name for your list. Tap the enter button on your mobile keypad to create your list. You can start adding items to your list immediately. Your custom list would be listed under **My Lists** in **Lists**. In a similar manner, you can tap on any of the default lists and items to them.

433. Alternatively, you can use your voice to create a list by saying, "Alexa, create a <list name> list." To add items to your list, you can say, "Alexa, add <item name> to my [shopping / to-do / <custom list name>] list," or "Alexa, remove <item name> from my [shopping / to-do / <custom list name>] list."

More useful invocations

434. To delete a list item: "Alexa, remove <item name or number> in my <list name>."

435. Add to your custom list: "Alexa, add to my <custom list name> list."

436. To find out what's on your list: "Alexa, show my [shopping / to-do / <custom list name>] list."

437. To clear a list: "Alexa, clear my [shopping / to-do / <custom list name>] list."

438. To **manage your list using a 3rd party list service**, go to **Settings** and tap on **Lists**. Select a list service from the list that appears and **Enable to Use** the skill. Follow through to configure the service. To disable the skill, go back to **Lists** under **Settings**, tap on it and **Disable Skill**.

Playing games on Your ES5

Catch funs with your Echo smart device with some cool Alexa games. To get started, you'll have to enable the skills — I mean your games, and it's easy too. As usual, to enable a skill in Alexa, launch the Alexa app and tap on **Skills & Games** from the **Menu**. Tap on **Game, Trivia & Accessories** and browse through the games there. Once you find something that you love, tap on **Enable Skill.**

439. Some recommendations include; Jeopardy, Price It Right, Twenty Questions, Bingo, Game Of Lists, Spelling Bee, Song Quiz, Screen Test, Millionaire Quiz Game, Code Guess, Letter Clutter, etc. To launch or play a game once enabled, say, "Alexa, open [or play] <skill name>."

440. **Tip:** You can enable **Twitch** to help you with updates on your favorite players or IRL channels. You can say, "Alexa, ask Twitch which player is playing <game name>," or "Alexa, ask Twitch to recommend an IRL channel."

Flash Briefings

You can hear news from popular broadcasters and news stations including video flashes from Alexa when you set up your Flash Briefings.

441. To setup your Flash Briefings in the Alexa app, go to **Settings** from the **Menu** ▤ then **Flash Briefings**. Toggle ON or enable available services listed, then tap on **Add Content** ⊕. On the ensuing screen, tap on the Search 🔍 button and begin searching your favorite Flash Briefing with specific skill name.

442. Some popular Flash Briefings skills include; NPR, Bloomberg, CBNC, Wall Street Journal, Fox News, Washington Post, BBC News, CNN, Reuters, MTV UK News, etc. Others include Ask Wxbrad (for weather information), Digg (for curated news), Curiosity Daily (for science and technology updates), Marketplace (for news in economics), Daily Tech Headlines (for tech news), Fox Sports (for latest sport news), etc.

Some useful invocation phrases:
443. To ask for a Flash Briefing, say, "Alexa, what's my Flash Briefing?"

444. To ask for specific Flash Briefing, say, "Alexa, what are my [News / Sport / Weather, etc.] Flash Briefings?"

445. To navigate stories, say, "Alexa, [next / previous / cancel]."

446. For video flash briefings, you can say, "Alexa, [pause / stop / resume / continue / next / previous]."

447. From a particular channel: "Alexa, play my flash briefings from <flash briefing source/skill name>." Example, "Alexa, play my flash briefings from CNBC." **Tip:** Enable the CNBC skill first by saying, "Alexa, enable CNBC."

448. Follow cards that appear on screen for full story.

Changing Background Photo

449. In the Alexa application, tap the **Menu** icon to see the full side menu then select

Settings. From Settings, select your ES5 from the list of devices. Scroll down to **Home Screen Background** and **Choose A Photo**. Browse and pick a photo from your phone then **Upload** it. This replaces your Echo Show background photo.

Simple Mathematics with Alexa

Alexa can handle simple Mathematics (especially for your kids) such as multiplication, basic addition, subtraction or division. Alexa can also give the value of Mathematical constants or help you with simple conversions (e.g., currency, metrics, etc.), e.g., *"Alexa, how much is 50 Pounds in US Dollars?"*

450. The skill, 1-2-3 Math can also help your kids to learn Math even faster. It tests one's ability to add, subtract, multiply, divide, compare, etc. It works in three modes: easy, medium & hard. You may need a Calculator to meet up with allotted time. To enable this skill, say, *"Alexa, enable one two three."*

Invocations to use 1-2-3 Math:

451. To have Alexa repeat the question again, say, "Alexa, [say again / repeat],"

452. To get clearer instructions, say, "Alexa, help."

453. To get your scores, say, "Alexa, score."

454. To change game level, say, "Alexa, change the level to [easy / medium / hard]."

Read Your eBooks or Listen to Audiobooks

455. Alexa can conveniently read Text-to-Speech supported eBooks in your Kindle Library. To get started, tap on the **Music & Book** icon located on the Alexa homepage. In the Kindle Library, you can see all your eBooks. Select any one and choose a device for it. Whether the book was shared with you, you purchased or borrowed them,

Alexa can attempt reading them for you. It doesn't matter if you've read the book from another device, Alexa can pick up from there. This is made possible by the Whispersync for Voice technology supported by Alexa.

Useful invocations for reading eBooks or listening to audiobooks:

Reading eBooks

456. To see your books: "Alexa, show my Kindle Books."

457. To start book reading: "Alexa, play <book title> from Kindle Library"

458. To control playback: "Alexa, [stop / pause / resume / skip."

459. To jump to another chapter: "Alexa, read <chapter number>."

Listening to audiobooks

460. Listening to an audiobook: "Alexa, read <book title>"

461. To control playback: "Alexa, [stop / pause / resume my book]"

462. To go backward or forward by 30 seconds: "Alexa, go back / go forward].

463. To jump to another chapter: "Alexa, [next / previous] chapter. Or "Alexa, go to chapter <#>."

464. Restart a chapter: "Alexa, restart."

465. Stop after time count: "Alexa, stop reading in <#> minutes" or "Alexa, stop reading in <#> hour."

466. Stop after time count: "Alexa, stop reading in [#] minutes" or "Alexa, stop reading in [#] hour."

467. To have Alexa read a title from Audible: "Alexa, read [book title] from Audible."

468. To get information about free books: "Alexa, what's free on Audible today?"

Alexa for Kids

Alexa is fun for the family. Allow the children also to have a feel of her as you do. You can enable any of the following skills for your kids.

469. Recommendations include; Christmas Kindness, the Magic Door, Spelling Bee, Ditty, Curiosity, Superheroes, Knock Knock Jokes, Short Bedtime Story, Cat Facts, Dog Facts, Dinosaur Facts, Guess the Number, Twenty Questions, State Capital Quiz, Earplay, Bingo, Laugh Box, Complibot, Pikachu Talk, Sheep Count, Kids News, Quick Snacks, 4A Fart, Panda Rescue, Sesame Street, Escape the Room, Freeze Dancers, See Say, Science Buddy, True or False, Eco Hacks, Heads Up, etc.

470. You can use this format to invoke any of these skills: "Alexa, open <skill name>" or "Alexa, start <skill name>."

Random Facts from Alexa

471. Simply say, "Alexa tell me some facts" or "Alexa, tell me some interesting things" and you'll be shocked with facts from Alexa.

472. Alternatively, you can enable a skill for random facts. To enable random facts skills, say, *"Alexa, [start / open / launch] Random Facts."* You can request for facts across categories such as money, random, Disney, weather, Dinosaur, number, food, today, world, etc. You can also enable additional extras with a premium subscription.

Get Medical Information from Alexa

473. Alexa continues to improve and becoming even more sophisticated. Now, you can ask Alexa some medical questions bordering on symptoms, causes and treatments from trusted sources such as Mayo Clinic, CDC, NIH, Disease Ontology Database, Wikipedia and Wikidata.

474. **Note:** Medical information provided by Alexa is only for informational purpose and should not be used as a standard for treatment. If you have medical emergency, get to a nearby hospital immediately or call your Doctor.

Get Information from Wikipedia

475. While you can do this through the Browser, you can also use your voice to fetch information from Wikipedia by saying, "Alexa, Wikipedia <subject>," e.g., "Alexa, Wikipedia Albert Einstein."

Information on Nearby Places: Businesses and Restaurants

Get information about shops, local restaurants, and other businesses. It's important that your address in Settings is correct and complete especially for this purpose. Alexa uses information mostly from Yelp to deliver on your requests.

476. To search for restaurants or businesses nearby: "Alexa, show [restaurants / businesses] close to me"

477. To see top-rated restaurants/businesses close to you: "Alexa, what top-rated [restaurants / businesses] are close to me?"

478. Get address of a restaurant/business close to you: "Alexa, find the address of [restaurants / businesses] close to me."

479. To get phone numbers of a [restaurant / business] close to you: "Alexa, find the phone number of a [restaurant / business] close to me."

480. To get their opening and closing hours: "Alexa, find the hours of a [restaurant / business] close to me."

Radio and Podcast

481. Listen to Radio and Podcast on News, Finance, Science, Tech & Design, Pop Culture, etc. Even when you don't have any specific podcast genre or Radio station, Alexa can recommend something to you. For Radio, you can say, "Alexa, recommend a radio station for me," or "Alexa, recommend a <genre> podcast for me." Where you know the title of the podcast, you can say, "Alexa, [show / play] the podcast <podcast title/name>."

Deleting Your Voice Recordings

482. Sometimes the Amazon Echo triggers inadvertently and starts recording sounds within its reach considering her sharp microphones. You may not know that you have recordings in Alexa history. This may not really be a factor, but if you feel the device must have recorded sensitive information then it becomes something to worry about.

483. To be on the safe side, you can choose to clear your Alexa history. To begin, go to **Settings** on your Alexa app and tap on **Alexa Account** then **History**. At **History**, you can see all your saved recordings. Go ahead and delete them one after the one. However, to delete everything at once, from your PC, log in to your Amazon account and go to **Content & Devices**. Click on **Your Devices** and select the **Alexa device** you want to erase all recordings then **Manage Voice Recordings**, choose the option to erase everything.

484. To find out what Alexa heard and recorded, say, "Alexa, what did you hear?"

485. To delete what she heard, say, "Alexa, delete everything I have just said" or "Alexa, delete what I said yesterday."

Turn off the screen

486. You can turn off the screen if you don't want someone to see what's showing. Turning the screen off is not shutting down the device completely but only putting it on sleep. To turn off the screen, you can say, "Alexa, turn

the screen off" or "Alexa, standby," then use the wake word to put it back on.

When to Restart / Reset Your ES5

487. A device reset is necessary if you want to sell or give your Echo device to someone else and hence, the need to clear your personal data. You can also reset the device if it becomes unresponsive or you want to correct a stubborn glitch that you can't fix through a restart. In any case, restarting the device is simple: pull off the plug from the power outlet and hold it for seconds then plug it back.

488. However, before performing a reset, note that there are two options to it: resetting to Factory Default but **retaining the Smart Home Device Connections** or resetting to **Factory Defaults** completely — clearing all settings and personal information. Whichever you choose to go for, say, "Alexa, go to Settings." You can also get to **Settings** by **swiping down** the device screen and selecting

Settings. At **Settings**, tap **Device Settings**, and then reset the device to any of the options explained above.

Alexa Skills — What are they?

What is Alexa Skill?

489. Alexa Skill is the brain behind the workings of external smart home devices or third-party applications in Amazon Alexa-enabled devices. In simple terms, Alexa Skill binds external smart home devices with your Echo Show [in this case]. You too can also come up with something, and then create an Alexa skill to make it work with your Echo device (Alexa Blueprint — How to Create Custom Skills for Alexa).

How to Enable a Skill

490. For Alexa Skills created by you, you can easily call the name of the Skill and tell Alexa

to enable it. However, for external smart home devices, you will need to install the companion app (where necessary) and enable the Skill in the Alexa app or through a voice command. After enabling a Skill, you can then use it as desired or discover a device that associate with it by saying, "Alexa, discover devices." Generally, to enable a Skill, simply say, "Alexa, enable <skill name>," e.g., "Alexa, enable Jeopardy." Alternatively, you can locate and manually enable a Skill via **Menu** ▤ => Skills & Games. Browse through the **Featured** or **All Categories** to find your desire Alexa Skill. Tap on the Skill and enable it.

491. To see a list of all Skills you've enabled, go to **Your Skills** tab on the **Skills & Games** page in the Alexa app. You can also say, "Alexa, open my skills" and follow up from there.

492. **Tips:** (1) After enabling a skill, you may still have to say "Alexa, open <skill name>" before you can start sending commands to it. (2) Most times, skills uses the format: "Alexa, ask <skill name> to …"

How to Disable a Skill

493. Tap on any skill and **Disable** it on **Your Skills** tab. Alternatively, use the format: *"Alexa, disable <Skill name>"* to disable any skill using your voice.

Alexa Blueprint—How to Create Custom Skills for Alexa

Alexa Blueprint is a service that enables users of Alexa powered devices to create skills for Alexa.

494. To create an Alexa skill, visit **blueprints.amazon.com** and log in to your account and supply necessary information about yourself then choose a template or blueprints for your custom skill. You can make a fairy tale, quiz game, etc. You can go through the Featured Blueprints to see what's available. Blueprints are also categorized.

495. Once you find a template that you'll love to work with, click on it to see more details on how to create something out of it.

Customizing a blueprint is easy and straightforward. Listen to the sample of the Blueprint and **Make Your Own**. Give your Blueprint a simple straight name. You can always come back to edit the **Skills You've Made** by clicking on the **Edit** button for your Skill. See option at the top of the Blueprint homepage.

496. Give minutes for your Skill to be ready. The system would notify you when it's time. Look out for a green notification message. Once **Ready to Use**, you can enable the skill for your device. For example, "Alexa, open My Trend," where 'My Trend' is your skill name.

497. You can also disable or delete a skill from your account via **Skills You've Made** if you are not comfortable with it.

How-to / Do-It-Yourself with Alexa

WikiHow holds great information on Do-It-Yourself, the skill when enable can answer all your how-to / DIY questions.

498.   To get started, enable the WikiHow skill by saying, "Alexa, enable WikiHow." Next, say, "Alexa, open WikiHow."

499.   **Tip:** (1) Think of any questions on how-to and ask WikiHow. To begin, say, "Alexa, open" and then ask your questions. (2) All questions should be in the format: "Alexa, ask WikiHow how to …" Example, "Alexa, ask WikiHow how to cook sausage roll."

Echo Show 5 in the Kitchen

One of the most interesting stuff about the Echo Show 5 is using it in the kitchen to help with cooking. The top Skill responsible for this is **Allrecipes**. You can easily enable Allrecipes by saying, "Alexa, enable Allrecipes."

501. Once you've enable a cooking skill, Alexa can search through the skill's database to deliver on your request. For instance, you want to prepare sausage roll, you can say, "Alexa, ask AllRecipes to show me how to make a sausage roll." This invocation would help her search through Allrecipes and then display search results related to preparing sausage rolls. Select from the result or say, "Alexa, show more" to see more search results. Once you've picked a recipe, you can tell Alexa to play the method or procedures ("Alexa, play recipe video). If you choose to play the video, the steps to prepare your sausage rolls is displayed on the screen. You can then scroll to see more.

502. Other recipe skills/services include; SideChef, Food Network, Recipedia, Good

Housekeeping, MyChef, OurGroceries, Instant Pot, Meal Idea, etc.

503. General invocation format: "Alexa, ask <recipe skill> for a <recipe name>," or "Alexa, ask <skill name> what I can make for [breakfast / lunch / dinner]."

Monitoring Your Home with Alexa Guard

504. The Alexa Guard feature is designed to watch out for emergencies and then trigger a smart alert to a connected mobile phone. Alexa Guard listens to alarms or glass breaks within the house and then triggers an alert. Such alert can contains an audio feed of the incident depending on what nature of Amazon Echo device you are using.

505. Alexa Guard can trigger the Drop In feature for live recording. It can also trigger your smart bulbs to switch on and off to make it appear as though there's someone in the house.

506. To get started with Alexa Guard, from the Alexa app, tap the **Menu** > **Settings** > **Guard** > **Set Up Guard** > **Add** — to listen to smart smoke alarm > **Add** — to listen to broken glass sound > **Add** — to light up your smart bulbs from time to time > **Enter Zip Code** > **Confirm**. Viola! You've just set up Alexa Guard in your home.

507. To get Alexa Guard to work, simply say, "Alexa, I'm leaving."

Mindful Meditation with Alexa

You want to do some meditations? Well, Alexa can help you with that using the Headspace skill. All you need to do is to link your Headspace account with Alexa; you can begin to enjoy free meditations on a daily basis as well as soothing music and sleeping single.

508. **Tip:** Having a paid membership enables you to access all that Headspace has to offer.

Meditation with Headspace works in the United States, United Kingdom, India, Canada, and Australia.

509. To begin, say, "Alexa, open Headspace" to enable the Headspace skill. Follow onscreen instructions to link your Headspace account. **Tip:** Get your Headspace login details ready.

510. Alternatively, open your Alexa app, tap **Menu** and then **Skills**. Search for and Enable Headspace.

511. Once ready for meditation, say, "Alexa, I am ready [to meditate / for bed]"

Troubleshooting the ES5
Inability to connect to WiFi

512. The common solution is turning off your Router and Echo device then putting them back on.

513. If the problem isn't fixed after trying (a) above, try to adjust the position of your Echo

Show away from devices that might be blocking or interfering with signals, e.g., microwaves, baby monitors, etc.

Difficulty in connecting Alexa to other smart devices

514. Check for compatibility of your smart device with your Echo. URL: **amazon.com/b?node=6563140011**

515. Check that the companion skill for your smart device is enabled in the Alexa app then try discovering the device by saying, "Alexa, discover devices."

516. Make sure your smart home device is on the same network with your Echo Show.

Echo Show 5 won't power

517. Check that the power adapter is still in good shape.

518. If "Yes" to [1] above, then you'll have to contact Amazon support. The Motherboard may be faulty.

Distorted Audio

519. The speaker might have been damage due to high volume and needs to be replaced.

Alexa won't understand me

520. If you are finding it difficult having Alexa understands your voice then you may need to take the voice training with Alexa. For more details, *see* "Teaching Alexa to always recognize your Voice."

Bluetooth devices won't pair up

521. The Echo Show supports the A2DP SNK and AVRCP Bluetooth Technology. Check your device if it matches with these technology.

522. Ensure that your Bluetooth's device battery is over 50% charged.

523. Unpair all Bluetooth devices (Settings > <Echo device name> > Bluetooth > Clear All Paired Devices) with your Echo Show and pair them back again ("*Alexa, pair devices,*" while setting your devices on pairing mode).

Music Streaming Service won't connect

524. Check your login details to make sure they are correct.

525. Reset your login details using a Computer on the Service Provider's website.

526. Make sure you set your mobile keypad to lowercase should the first letter of your password is not a capital letter. Again, check that there is not empty space before/after your username.

527. Use a computer and link your music service account from **alexa.amazon.com**

528. Reboot your router.

529. Update your Alexa app.

530. Make sure both your Amazon and mobile device are connected to the same network.

531. Restart your Echo Show by unplugging it from mains and plugging it again.

532. Restart Alexa app.

533. Disable and enable music service app on Alexa.

Background picture won't rotate

534. When you set your Home Screen Background to Prime Photos, the background photo supposed to change at interval but if it gets stuck, try to restart the Echo Show by unplugging it from mains and plugging it back after 10-20 seconds. If the problem persists, contact Amazon Support. You may wish to request for a replacement.

Video / voice calls not working

535. Use a supported/compatible device to install Alexa app or make a call. Use Android 5.0 and later on a compatible device.

536. Check your connection to the internet as well as your signal quality. Signal quality must be strong.

537. Turn off your internet connection, wait for 30 seconds or more and put it back on.

538. You can also restart your Android device.

539. Pull off the power adapter from the Echo device and plug back after 3 seconds while restarting the internet connection.

540. Confirm that the contact you are trying to call is listed under **Contacts** in **Communication** in the Alexa app. If not listed, sign out and sign in to the Alexa app via **Settings**. For Fire Tablet, go to Account settings, deregister and register the device again.

Alexa skill isn't working

541. Disable and enable the skill again then restart your Alexa device.

No Audio

542. The cables connecting the speakers might have been disconnected. See a technician.

Camera not working

543. Check to see that you've not used the shutter to cover the camera.

544. Contact Amazon support for unit replacement.

Call Amazon Customer Care on Alexa

545. "Alexa, call customer service."

Claim your free eBook

Send an email to:

siggny1@gmail.com

Thank you for your purchase.

Printed in Great Britain
by Amazon

52457422R00095